Travellers

PARIS

BY
ELISABETH MORRIS

Produced by
Thomas Cook Publishing

Written by Elisabeth Morris

Original photography by Anthony Souter and Ken Patterson

Edited and designed by Laburnum Technologies Pvt Ltd, C-533 Triveni Apts, Sheikh Sarai Phase 1, New Delhi 110017

Published by Thomas Cook Publishing A division of Thomas Cook Holdings Ltd

PO Box 227, The Thomas Cook Business Park, Units 19–21, Coningsby Road, Peterborough PE3 8XX, United Kingdom E-mail: books@thomascook.com www.thomascookpublishing.com

ISBN: 1-841572-41-1

Managing Director: Kevin Fitzgerald

Publisher: Donald Greig

Series Consultant: Vivien Stone

Printed and bound in Spain by: Grafo Industrias Gráficas, Basauri

Cover: The Louvre and glass pyramid. Photograph supplied by Pictures Colour Library.
Inside cover: photographs supplied by Spectrum Colour Library

CD manufacturing services provided by business interactive ltd, Rutland, UK

Contents

Introduction

Fluctuat nec mergitur, 'she is buffeted by the waves but she does not sink', has been the city's proud motto for over four centuries . . . and still holds true today. Through revolutions, wars, foreign occupation and, above all, redevelopment, Paris has remained true to her image for generation after generation of enthusiastic admirers.

The sheer beauty of the capital conquers first-time visitors. A harmonious ensemble of splendid monuments and elegant domestic architecture provides a unique impression of unity; moreover, everything seems to be in its rightful place, from the Madeleine matching the National Assembly across the place de la Concorde to the unobtrusive place Dauphine at the tip of the Ile-de-la-Cité. Yet subtle planning and inspired improvisation are constantly remodelling the seemingly perfect image of Paris, and while pessimists predict that 'it will never be the same again', these innovations are being enthusiastically accepted by Parisians and outsiders alike. To give but three examples: the Eiffel Tower, which raised such an outcry when it was built more than a hundred years ago, has become the most familiar landmark of the city; the controversial Centre Pompidou is now the most visited monument; and the Louvre would already seem incomplete without its pyramid.

However, beauty alone does not explain the attraction of Paris for so many. One could argue in favour of its vast cultural wealth, its *haute couture,* the infinite variety of its cuisine, or its reputation in the field of entertainment. However, its magical appeal is due mainly to an undefinable charm that seems to spring quite unexpectedly from the many facets of everyday life. Ordinary details, no matter how trivial, suddenly seem to acquire a new dimension: it could be a quaint-looking kiosk on a street corner; a whiteglobed street lamp in the middle of a tiny square; an old-fashioned shopfront; the *bouquinistes* (second-hand bookstalls) in the morning mist; or just an evocative street name like the rue du Chat-qui-Pêche (fishing cat street).

Full of contradictions, Paris never ceases to surprise: at once compact and spacious, it can be in turn pompous and modest, cheap and outrageously expensive, enthralling and infuriating, depending on the place and time of day.

'Nothing can be compared to Paris.'
From a popular 14th-century ballad by
EUSTACHE DESCAMPS

'This city without an equal, this summary of France.'
JEAN BERTAUT (16th century)

'Paris is well worth a Mass!'
HENRI IV, when he converted to Catholicism to become King of France

'Whoever looks into the depths of Paris gets dizzy. Nothing so fantastic, nothing so tragic, nothing so superb.'
VICTOR HUGO

'As an artist, a man has no home save in Paris.'
FRIEDRICH NIETZSCHE

The Conciergerie, massive yet graceful

History

52 BC	Romans conquer the island; the settlement prospers and spreads to the left bank.	**1420**	Height of the Hundred Years War: the English occupy Paris.
c.280	Barbarians raid city. The Parisii flee to the island.	**1430**	Henry VI of England crowned king of France.
c.360	Paris gets its name.	**1436**	Charles VII recaptures the city.
451	Attila's Huns attack. The young Geneviève predicts the town will be spared; she is later made the city's patron saint.	**1546**	New Renaissance palace at the Louvre begun.
508	The first Christian king of the Franks, Clovis, makes Paris his capital.	**1572**	Saint-Bartholomew's Day massacre. Several thousand Huguenots die.
7th century	King Dagobert is buried in the Basilica of Saint-Denis.	**1578–1604**	The Pont-Neuf is built.
		Late-17th century	Louis XIV moves to Versailles, founds Les Invalides.
1163	Notre-Dame Cathedral begun by Maurice de Sully, Bishop of Paris.	**c.1760**	Louis XV commissions the Ecole Militaire, the Panthéon, and the place de la Concorde.
1180	King Philippe-Auguste orders a new city wall and the Louvre fortress.	**1789**	The fall of the Bastille (14th July) marks the beginning of the French Revolution.
1215	The first university in France founded in Paris.		
1253	The Sorbonne founded.	**1792**	Proclamation of the First Republic.
1364	Charles V starts a new wall around Paris and the Bastille.	**1793**	Louis XVI guillotined. Louvre Museum opens.

1804	Napoleon is crowned Emperor in Notre-Dame.	**1940**	Paris bombed and occupied by Germans.
Early-19th century	The Arc de Triomphe is built, also theatres and shopping arcades.	**1944**	Paris is liberated.
		1958	Work starts on La Défense.
1848	Louis Napoleon, nephew of Napoleon I, elected first President of the Second Republic.	**1968**	'May Events' put barricades in the streets.
1852–70	Baron Haussmann remodels Paris.	**1969**	The Halles central food market is moved to Rungis, outside Paris.
1870–71	Third Republic is proclaimed. The Paris Commune crushed at the expense of some of the town's finest monuments.	**1977**	The first mayor of Paris since 1871 is elected and the Centre Pompidou is opened.
1889	Eiffel Tower built for the Exposition Universelle.	**1986**	The Orsay Museum and the Cité des Sciences at La Villette are inaugurated.
1900	First métro line opened. Paris becomes an international centre of fashion and entertainment. Montmartre witnesses the birth of modern art.	**1989**	A series of celebrations, including the inauguration of the Bastille Opera and of the Grande Arche at La Défense, commemorate the bicentenary of the fall of the Bastille.
1914	Paris is saved from German invasion by the Battle of the Marne.	**1996**	Mitterand officially opens the Bibliothèque Nationale de France.
1937	The Palais de Chaillot and Tokyo built for the Exposition Universelle.	**1998**	French World Cup Victory.

The City

Paris is situated in northern France, at the centre of a vast natural chalk basin drained by the River Seine and its numerous tributaries, including the Marne and the Oise.

The Ile-de-France

The area surrounding Paris is, as its name suggests, the very 'heart' of France. This privilege goes back to the 6th century, when the region already formed the core of the kingdom of the Franks. Rich agricultural land, green valleys, beautiful forests, a temperate climate, easy communications, and the presence of the capital in its centre secured its supremacy over the rest of the country.

However, the division of the whole French territory into some 90 *départements* at the end of the 18th century made the region's limits rather difficult to define. It was, for a long time, vaguely referred to as the 'Paris Region' and the name Ile-de-France seemed to be relegated to history books.

In 1976, France was divided into 22 regions, each including several *départements,* and Paris Region was officially given back its original name of Ile-de-France. The region comprises Paris and seven other *départements* clustering round the capital.

Since the introduction of gradual decentralisation over the past 20 years, the region has been governed by a Conseil Régional consisting of 197 councillors elected for a period of six years, assisted by a Comité économique et social, which advises on specific projects.

Economy

The Ile-de-France is an area of great economic wealth, modelled by its illustrious past but definitely looking to the future. It covers only 2.2 per cent of France, but accommodates a fifth of the population and has no fewer than five 'new towns'. It is by far the most densely populated of all the regions, and contributes over a quarter of the gross national product.

The population of Paris has, like that of many large towns has, with the influx of immigrants become so cosmopolitan that the notion of a 'true Parisian' may seem like a myth! But visitors need have no fear . . . the true Parisian is still very real.

He or she may originally have come from a different part of France, or even from abroad, but once adopted by Paris, becomes a true Parisian: hurrying along the pavements and the métro corridors, hurrying to work and hurrying back home again in the evening, hurrying through life, in fact . . . not particularly amiable, especially if at the wheel of a car, but quick-witted and able to enjoy life intensely for a fleeting moment.

Nothing shocks or even surprises Parisians, and they would even be very tolerant . . .if there was time!

Commerce, transport, and service industries are the most developed economic activities and account for nearly three quarters of the jobs. The industrial sector is almost equally strong and produces a quarter of the total industrial wealth of the country. Power generation, electronics, publishing and printing, pharmaceutical products, car- and ship-building, as well as food, are the main industries.

Agriculture, on the other hand, although far from negligible and highly efficient, is economically very much in the background and specialises more and more in the intensive production of cereals, flowers, and ornamental plants.

The City

Neatly enclosed within a mostly efficient ring road, which can be highly frustrating during the rush hour, Paris, dominated by the Seine, covers an area of a mere 105sq km.

The population of the capital has now stabilised at just over 2 million inhabitants. During the past 15 years, the tendency has been for people to move out of Paris and settle in other *départements* of the region, which Parisians call *la banlieue* (suburbs). The areas surrounding the capital are officially referred to as *la petite couronne* (the close suburbs) and *la grande couronne* (the outskirts).

The Sacré-Coeur is visible from most parts of the city

Governance

Paris owes its unique economic and cultural drive to its long-standing role as capital of France. It took an active part in all the major events of French history, suffering greatly during the more sombre periods of revolution and war, but always recovering and regaining its vitality, wit and artistic taste.

Palais de Justice. Its beauty belies its turbulent history

The Corridors of Power

Today, there are in France three distinct components of government: the parliament, the government, and the president.

Parliament consists of two houses: the Assemblée Nationale, elected for five years, sits in the Palais Bourbon facing the place de la Concorde; it discusses and votes on the laws, while the Sénat, elected for nine years and housed in the Palais du Luxembourg, has a purely advisory role.

The government is made up of the prime minister, chosen by the president, and a variable number of ministers. Together they are answerable to the Assemblée Nationale for their policies. The prime minister resides in the Hôtel Matignon, in the Faubourg St-Germain.

The Président de la République is elected for seven years; he chooses the prime minister and presides over cabinet meetings. He is head of the armed forces, has considerable powers in foreign affairs, ensures the independence of the judiciary and may be granted special powers in exceptional circumstances. The Palais de l'Elysée is the president's official residence. Helping to turn the wheels of power, the

political parties and the trade unions are all based in the capital, as are the national newspapers.

Finally, one must not forget the people of Paris who have always shown great interest in the running of national affairs, and take an active part in decision-making through frequent street demonstrations and gatherings in public squares.

Embassies from countries all over the world have long been established in the capital, which is also the seat of major international organisations such as UNESCO (United Nations Educational, Scientific, and Cultural Organisation) and OECD (Organisation for Economic Cooperation and Development). Paris has lately become the most sought-after centre of international congress in the world, overtaking London and Brussels.

Town and Département

At local government level, Paris has, since 1977, enjoyed the unique privilege of being at once a *commune* and a *département*. As a *commune* or municipality, it has an elected mayor chosen by the municipal council; elections are held every six years. The *commune* of Paris is divided into 20 *arrondissements,* each having its own mayor, and working closely with the central municipal authority, which meets at the Hôtel de Ville.

When the Ile-de-France region came into being, the Seine *département,* of which Paris was the main town, and several *départements* surrounding the capital were remodelled, and new ones created: with a fifth of the region's total population, Paris became a *département* in its own right, administered by the Conseil de Paris.

Decentralisation

The endowment on the local authority of real powers proved beneficial to the city as it enabled the municipality and the state to share the responsibility for the capital's great architectural heritage and to initiate daring futuristic projects aimed at maintaining Paris's position as one of the major European cities of the modern world. Even if everything has not always gone smoothly, the results so far are stunning: whole districts, which had become derelict, have been restored (like the Marais), or completely rebuilt (like the Halles), but their traditions have been preserved. At the same time, the renovation of eastern districts, neglected for far too long, was inspired by bold town planning principles with astonishing results: thus La Villette is fast becoming a major cultural attraction.

Excitement over the changing face of Paris is not about to abate, especially since communications and the environment have become very controversial issues in local politics.

The classically styled Assemblée Nationale, where the lawmaking body of the French parliament sits

Culture

Foreigners usually expect to discover in Paris the very essence of French culture and they are right to a certain extent, although provincial French people would not agree, however proud they may be of their capital. Wit, elegance, and energy are all to be found in Paris. Parisians are aware that the rest of France is watching them and have always considered this a worthwhile challenge. As a result, they have developed a strong need to innovate, as well as a tremendous drive to achieve their goals.

A big sign for a big show in Montparnasse

The Changing Face of Paris

A great deal of systematic restoration work has been undertaken, and a number of buildings have acquired a renewed and restored usefulness. The magnificent but obsolete Gare d'Orsay has been renovated in an imaginative way and turned into an art museum, while a glass pyramid lets daylight into the underground entrance hall of the Louvre Museum. The last of IM Pei's grand plan for this area was completed in 1999, at a cost of over $1 billion, making the Louvre the world's largest museum.

Moreover, for the first time, whole districts have been saved from dereliction with the help of modern techniques of conservation: in the Marais, for example, the splendour of the past has come to life again. At the same time, vast architectural projects initiated in the latter half of the 20th century ensured cultural continuity. Some of them, such as the Forum des Halles, La Villette, and La Défense, are particularly striking.

A Certain Way of Life

Parisians may be fond of new ideas, but they are also conservative, and their lifestyle reflects this constant conflict between innovation and tradition. Paris has always been a compact city and Parisians have become used to living in cramped conditions, in blocks of flats that traditionally have six storeys and a concierge (caretaker) on the ground floor. Therefore, street life is important to them: local bistros, brasseries and cafés are a favourite meeting place throughout the day. Open-air markets, where people from different generations and social backgrounds mingle in a colourful display of exuberance, have remained the focal point of many districts.

Furthermore, Parisians have a reputation for trendsetting: a district suddenly becomes fashionable and everyone wants to live in it. This phenomenon is also apparent in two other important aspects of Parisian life – clothing and food, where there is a definite cosmopolitan influence.

Subtle Changes

The traditional way of life is gradually changing as the fabric of the population itself alters: the number of workers in high-tech industries, members of the professional classes, and artists is increasing rapidly, while the contrast between wealthy western districts and poorer eastern areas is disappearing. At the same time, the pace of living has considerably quickened, inevitably damaging personal contacts. On the other hand, Paris is becoming truly cosmopolitan, which has brought greater cultural variety to the Parisian scene.

Culture for Everyone

Paris is as much as ever a melting pot of artistic creation and a place where one can never tire of being a spectator. Music, drama, and the visual arts are taught at various levels, from the municipal schools to the national *conservatoires*.

Paris is also the place to visit for those who do not take an active part in culture but thrive on it. There are, of course, prestigious opera houses, concert halls, and theatres, but there are also free concerts in many churches all over town, and avant-garde plays in tiny, obscure theatres.

In addition to their permanent collections, museums and art galleries organise temporary exhibitions. The number of libraries is increasing rapidly, and there are still a record number of cinemas in spite of fierce competition from television. Also, this brief review of the cultural scene would be incomplete without a special mention of two great multi-purpose cultural centres: the Pompidou Centre, and the music and science complex at La Villette.

The stately 16th-century Louvre, now served by its glass-pyramid information centre

Festivals and Events

Festivals stem from an ancient tradition, but their number has greatly increased in recent years and they have developed from spontaneous, regular gatherings into elaborate forms of entertainment aimed at occasional visitors as well as local residents. Below are some of the regular highlights.

Fireworks celebrate the Nuit de la St-Jean

IN PARIS

Juin à Paris XVIe *June*
Concerts, tours, and plays in the 16th *arrondissement. Tel: 01 40 72 16 25.*

Festival 'Foire St-Germain' *June*
Theatre, music, exhibitions, and an antiques fair in the 6th arrondissement (St-Germain-des-Prés). Venues: the Mairie, 78 rue Bonaparte; the place St-Sulpice; the Hôtel de la Monnaie; 11 quai de Conti. *Tel: 01 43 29 61 04.*

Festival Chopin *mid-June–mid-July*
Concerts and recitals. Orangerie de Bagatelle, Bois de Boulogne, 75016. *Tel: 01 45 00 22 19.*

Festival de la Butte Montmartre
June & July
Theatre, music and dance. Check Tourist Office, *tel: 08 36 68 31 12.*

Festival Musique en l'Ile
July–September
Classical music. Eglise St-Louis-en-l'Ile, 19 bis rue St-Louis-en-l'Ile, 75004, métro: Pont-Marie; Left Bank, church of St-Germain-des-Prés, place St-Germain-des-Prés, 75006, métro: St-Germain-des-Prés. *Tel: 01 44 62 00 55.*

Paris, Quartier d'Eté
mid-July–mid-August
Festival of popular entertainment, with venues spread across the capital. *Tel: 01 44 94 98 00.*

Festival d'Automne
mid-September–end December
Music, dance, plays, and special exhibitions. *Tel: 01 53 45 17 00.*

Festival d'Art Sacré de la Ville de Paris *October–November*
Church music at church venues. *Tel: 01 45 08 55 25.*

Festival de Jazz de Paris
end October – beginning November
In various halls. *Tel: 01 47 83 84 06.*

Festival de Cinema en Plein Air
July & August
Tel: 01 40 03 75 75.

Musique Coté Jardin *May–September*
Tel: 08 20 00 75 75.

La Villette Jazz Festival
end June–beginning July
At Cité de la Musique. *Tel: 01 40 03 75 75.*

IN ILE-DE-FRANCE
Contact the Comité Régional du Tourisme d'Ile-de-France, *tel: 01 42 60 28 62,* for events in the Paris region.

St-Denis *June*
A festival of music.

Versailles *end May–end June*
Festival of instrumental music and opera in the Opéra Royal at the château.

Fontainebleau *July & August*
Concerts are given in the castle.

Parc de Sceaux *July–September*
Saison Musicale d'Eté gives concerts in the Orangerie.

Abbaye de Royaumont
May, June, September, & October
Concerts take place in abbey buildings.

St-Germain-en-Laye *September*
International festival in honour of the composer Claude Debussy.

Suresnes *1st weekend October*
8km west of Paris, a wine festival celebrates *les vendanges.*

Rueil-Malmaison *November*
Festival International du Film d'Histoire devoted to historical films.

FAIRS AND SPECIAL EVENTS
Foire du Trône *April & May*
A funfair in the Bois de Vincennes.

Fête de la Musique *21 June*
In the 20 *arrondissements* of Paris.
Tel: 01 42 76 40 40.

Nuit de la St-Jean *24 June*
Impressive fireworks display in the gardens of the Sacré-Coeur.

La Fête Nationale *13 July*
A huge open-air ball on the place de la Bastille, followed by a military parade along the Champs Elysées on 14 July in the morning and fireworks in the evening at the Trocadéro.

Fête des Tuileries *beginning July–mid-August, & in December*
Funfair in the Tuileries gardens.

Fête à Neu Neu *September*
Funfair in the Bois de Boulogne.

ART EXHIBITIONS
Salon de Mars *end March*
Antiquities, primitive and modern art on the Esplanade du Champ de Mars, 75007.

Les Cinq Jours de l'Objet Extraordinaire *late May*
A display of antiques by dealers of the Carré Rive Gauche, 75007.

Foire Internationale d'Art Contemporain *end October*
International contemporary art at the Grand Palais, avenue Winston Churchill, 75008.

Salon d'Automne *late October/early November*
Paintings, sculptures, photographs, and architecture at the Grand Palais.

Salon des Artistes Indépendants
after Salon d'Automne
Art exhibitions with different themes.

Impressions

'Paris is like an ocean; you can try to fathom it but you will never know its real depth.'

HONORÉ DE BALZAC

When to Go

In summer Paris belongs to the tourists. If you are looking for authenticity, August is the worst month as the city is deserted by Parisians, cultural activities are at a low ebb, quite a few restaurants and shops are closed and, on top of it all, the weather can be uncomfortably humid.

Winter has a certain charm, with statues and monuments looking stark through the leafless trees, but the days are short.

Directional signage is clear and highly visible.

Crowds in the streets reach their peak at Christmas time, a particularly lively period. January, with its traditional sales, is a good time for shopping.

However, late spring and early autumn are, on the whole, the most exciting seasons in which to visit Paris: in springtime, parks and gardens are a haven of freshness, while the long warm evenings invite you to stroll along the Seine or watch the sun set, the Arc de Triomphe ablaze. There is a holiday spirit in the air which brings smiles and humour into everyday conversation.

On the other hand, autumn marks the start of the season, *la rentrée* as the French call it: theatres and opera houses re-open, major exhibitions are announced, new trends in fashion are set, and children go back to school; moreover, Parisians are at their friendliest after their holidays spent away from the capital.

THOMAS COOK'S PARIS

Thomas Cook undertook his first-ever trip abroad to the Paris Exhibition in 1855. Because he couldn't get a concession on the Channel crossing, he went from Harwich to Brussels, down the Rhine to Strasbourg, and then overland to Paris. The party included four unaccompanied sisters who, although criticised for their daring, felt they could venture anywhere escorted by Mr Cook. (Cook's subsequent tours were heavily patronised by single women, whose travel horizons would otherwise have been limited by Victorian ideas of propriety.)

The total cost of the first trip, including expenses, was estimated by one of the sisters as £10. Paris became a favourite destination for Cook's parties, and the Thomas Cook's guidebook to Paris became a standard guide until the outbreak of World War II.

Lost? Find help at handy roadside maps

Getting Around

On arrival, you might take a taxi and be whirled round the place Charles-de-Gaulle, which continues to be referred to as l'Etoile. This can be a hair-raising experience, but you will quickly come to terms with it when you realise that the *priorité à droite* (priority to vehicles coming from the right) really works – most of the time, anyway! From then on the pace is set, and you begin to get the feel of the place.

If you are driving to Paris, you will soon discover that a car is not the best means to explore the French capital because of the volume of traffic and the time restrictions on parking. Therefore, your best course of action is to leave your car in a long-term car park (ask your hotel for information on the nearest one) and take to the streets.

Walking is by far the best way to visit the centre as distances are manageable and there are no hills. However, sooner or later, you will need to use some form of public transport. Paris is a densely populated, relatively compact city, but careful planning has provided it with wide avenues and two main thoroughfares along the Seine.

Finding your Bearings

Central Paris is relatively small and some of the familiar landmarks act as beacons: the Sacré-Coeur Basilica on top of Montmartre is due north, the Eiffel Tower is to the west, and the Montparnasse Tower dominates the southern part of town. Getting hold of a detailed map should be your first move. All street signs show which *arrondissement* you are in, and if you look these up in the index of your Paris street plan, it will even give you the nearest métro.

The Champs Elysées, leading to the Tuileries

AREAS OF PARIS

The areas situated on either side of the Seine have acquired their own character, but there is a distinction dear to the heart of Parisians between the Right Bank on the north side and the Left Bank in the south. It goes back to the Middle Ages, when the growing city started to spread along the banks of the river.

The Rive Gauche, or Left Bank, became the students' headquarters and has since been the favourite haunt of a lively bohemian society. The Latin Quarter, St-Germain-des-Prés, and Montparnasse have all been favoured by intellectuals at different times. Meanwhile, the Rive Droite, or Right Bank, traditionally conservative, has watched, sometimes with indulgence, sometimes with annoyance and even

A melting pot of cuisine and culture

downright anger, the antics going on across the river. A centre of business and commerce, it prides itself on having all the major department stores and *haute couture* boutiques (*see* Fashion, *pp150–51*).

Arrondissements

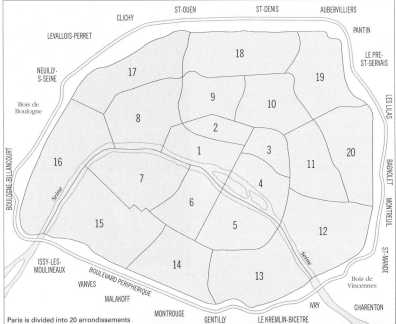

Paris is divided into 20 arrondissements

Even Montmartre, at one time renowned as the poor artists' quarter, has acquired a definite respectability and been overrun by tourists, while the authenticity of the red-light district of Pigalle, at the bottom of the hill, has almost disappeared.

Where to Go

You might find the following suggestions helpful when choosing a walk or an area to visit.

If you like medieval architecture and enchanting river settings, go to the Ile-de-la-Cité and the Ile St-Louis.

If you feel like taking it easy and mingling with a young crowd, aim for the Latin Quarter or St-Germain-des-Prés and watch the world go by from one of the lively cafés on the way.

If you are feeling energetic enough to take on monumental Paris, walk up the Champs Elysées or experience the thrill of admiring the city from the top of the Eiffel Tower.

If you enjoy shopping in a grand way, the Madeleine/Opéra area is the ideal choice, but if you wish to meet trendy young people, then go to Les Halles and Beaubourg.

If discreet elegance is what appeals to you, and you enjoy going round the art galleries, the Marais is where you want to be.

If you like modern architecture, take the métro to La Villette or the RER (see p20) to La Défense.

And if a desire for La Bohème compels you to go to Montmartre, ignore the artists on the Place du Tertre and pause to admire the view from the Sacré-Coeur.

Coping with the Weather

On a rainy day, the main cultural centres like La Villette and the Centre National d'Art et de Culture Georges Pompidou offer varied activities for all ages, as well meals and refreshments; so do large shopping centres like the Forum des Halles.

On the other hand, the department stores in the boulevard Haussmann are so close that you can go from one to the other without getting wet . . . and why not take the opportunity to discover one of the lovely shopping arcades near the Palais-Royal, or stroll among the 250 boutiques of the Louvre des Antiquaires (see p148).

Fancy meeting you here: place St-Sulpice

Public Transport

The métro, the RER, and the buses are part of a very efficient system. The métro, short for *métropolitain*, is an underground network of 15 lines covering the city within the *périphérique*; trains are frequent, stations are close to one another, and there is one flat fare throughout. You can either buy tickets in lots of 10 (a *carnet*) or get a *Paris-Visite* pass for unlimited travel anywhere for a specified number of days; you can combine it with a *Carte Musée-Monuments* (museum pass).

Maps of the whole network are posted outside stations and on platforms. You can change from one line to another at intersection points by following the sign *correspondance*. The métro runs daily from 5.30am to 12.30am; buses from 6.30am to either 9pm or 1am (*see p188* for more information on transport).

Travelling on the métro can be hectic, especially during the rush hour. A journey by bus, on the other hand, is usually an enjoyable experience, but don't forget to allow extra time and to ring the bell when you want to get off. The same tickets are used on buses and on the métro, but you may need two on the bus depending on the length of your journey.

Route finders, which look like cash dispensers, are called SITU. They are programmed to work out the quickest way to any destination by one or several means of transport, including walking.

The RER (Réseau Express Régional) is a suburban network of fast trains linked to the métro. The flat-fare system applies only within the city boundaries. The RER is a favoured means of transport between Orly airport and the centre of Paris. It has reduced the travelling time to about half an hour.

Within the Périphérique

Batobus

'Riverbuses' operate from April to September between the Eiffel Tower and the Hôtel de Ville, stopping at the Musée d'Orsay, the Louvre, and Notre-Dame.

Taxis

The best place to get one is from a *Tête de station* (taxi-rank). Drivers accept a maximum of three or four passengers and expect a tip of at least 10 per cent.

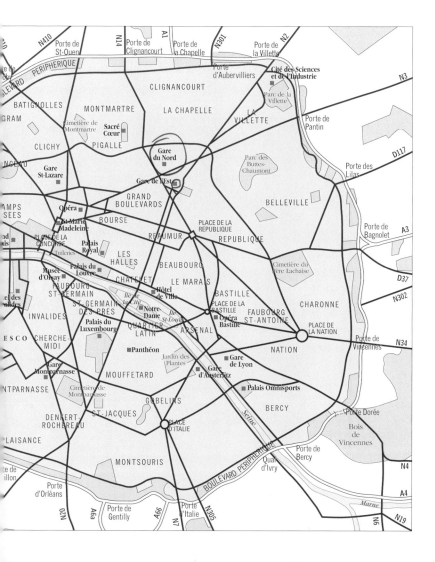

Paris Métro

Arc de Triomphe

The Arc de Triomphe has, like the Eiffel Tower, a magnetic appeal for visitors from all over the world. This can, to a large extent, be explained by its exceptional situation at the top of a hill, almost halfway between the Louvre and La Défense. Its square outline, easily spotted from afar, is well defined against the sky by day and illuminated by night.

As much a symbol of France as the Eiffel Tower

Thirty Years to Build ...
Commissioned in 1806 by Napoleon as a tribute to his Grande Armée, it is the largest triumphal arch ever built in the pure tradition of Roman architecture. The design was that of architect Jean Chalgrin. However, work progressed slowly (it took two years to lay the foundations!). Chalgrin died in 1811, and the construction of the arch almost came to a halt after the fall of Napoleon. It was finally completed in 1836.

The Arch Today
In 1840, the hearse carrying Napoleon's remains passed, quite appropriately, under the arch on its way to Les Invalides. Then, in 1920, the Unknown Soldier was buried beneath it, under a plain slab, and, since 11 November 1923, a remembrance ceremony has been held every year.

The flame is rekindled every evening at 6.30pm. On special occasions, a huge flag floats beneath the arch to splendid effect.

Viewed from a Distance
The arch is 50m high, 45m wide, and 22m thick. Of the four massive sculptures on the façades, only the one by François Rude has become famous for its bold inspiration. Known as La Marseillaise, it depicts the departure in 1792 of the volunteers, spurred on by a winged figure representing France.

Smaller reliefs on the façades and the sides feature victories won during the 1789 Revolution and the First Empire; a frieze by Rude and five other sculptors runs all round the arch. Along the top runs a row of shields inscribed with the names of victories won by Napoleon's Grande Armée.

GLORIOUS AND SOMBRE MOMENTS

In 1885, Victor Hugo, France's most popular man of letters, lay in state beneath the arch before being buried in the Panthéon.

On 14 July 1919, the allied armies celebrated victory by marching through the arch.

In 1940, the German army marched past it, greeted only by deadly silence.

In 1944, General de Gaulle was given a riotous welcome.

On 14 July 1989, the arch was the focal point of the joyous national celebrations for the bicentenary of the 1789 Revolution.

A Closer View

A subway leads from the northern pavement of the Champs Elysées to the base of the arch. Underneath, the names of hundreds of generals are inscribed on the walls: those who died in action are underlined. It is worth climbing to the platform on top of the arch by means of the lift or stairs. The perfectly symmetrical place de l'Etoile and the 12 avenues radiating from it offer a stunning view. To the west is the vast modern complex of La Défense. The small museum houses an exhibition explaining the construction of the arch, as well as the main events connected with it; there is also a video show in French and English.

Place Charles-de-Gaulle

It used to be called place de l'Etoile because of its star shape, until it was renamed after General de Gaulle; but here tradition dies hard and l'Etoile it remains in the hearts of all Parisians even now.

Over 100 years ago, Haussmann remodelled it and built elegant Neo-Classical mansions all round. The 120-m wide avenue Foch is the most exclusive residential street in Paris; among its illustrious inhabitants were the Duke and Duchess of Windsor.
Tel: 01 55 37 73 77. Open: daily 9.30am–11pm (winter 10am–10.30pm). Admission charge. Métro: Charles-de-Gaulle-Etoile. Access by subway from the north side of the Champs Elysées.

Nearby
Flower market on place des Ternes, FNAC hi-fi centre in avenue des Ternes, shopping arcades along the Champs Elysées.

The Arc de Triomphe floodlit at night

Walk: The Champs Elysées

This symbol of French elegance and glamour offers a unique and thrilling view that sweeps uphill to the Arc de Triomphe.

Allow 2 hours.

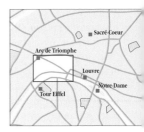

Start from place de la Concorde (métro Concorde).

1 Champs Elysées

The avenue was designed in the 17th century as a royal way leading out of Paris towards Versailles. Later, it became extremely fashionable to be seen driving along it in a horse-drawn carriage. In recent years, the Champs Elysées has been the scene of all major national celebrations, such as the bicentenary of the 1789 Revolution and, of course, the march past on 14 July.

Start walking along the main avenue.

2 Concorde to the Rond-Point

The paved avenue is lined with green open spaces planted with chestnut trees after the English fashion. The romantic alleys lead to half-concealed pavilions such as those occupied by the American Embassy and the Espace Cardin on the right-hand side.

Walk through the gardens on the left, and turn right along the Cours La Reine, then right again into avenue Winston Churchill.

3 Petit Palais

Like the Grand Palais facing it, the Petit Palais was built of stone and steel for the 1900 Exposition Universelle, and now houses the art collections of the city of Paris: Greek, Roman, and Egyptian art; medieval and Renaissance objects, books, and enamels; 16th- and 17th-century Dutch and Flemish paintings; 18th- century furniture and tapestries; and19th-century French paintings by masters such as Delacroix and Cézanne. *Closed for renovation till 2003.*

4 Grand Palais

In this imposing, glass-roofed building, adorned with an Ionic colonnade and elaborate sculptures, major art exhibitions are traditionally held, and the long queues winding outside this temple of culture are a familiar sight. At the back is the **Palais de la Découverte**, once a very popular science museum, but now overshadowed by the ultra-modern Cité des Sciences at La Villette. *Tel: 01 44 13 17 17. Open: 10am–8pm (10pm Wed). Cross the Champs Elysées and continue along avenue de Marigny.*

5 Palais de l'Elysée

On your left, at the corner of the avenue Gabriel, a stamp market is held on Thursdays and Sundays. Further along on the right is the Palais de l'Elysée, built in 1718, which counts among its famous owners the Marquise de

Tomb of the Unknown Soldier, Arc de Triomphe

Pompadour and Napoleon's sister Caroline. Since 1873 it has been the official residence of the president.
Turn left into rue du Faubourg-St-Honoré, lined with shops, then left again into avenue Matignon.

6 Rond-Point des Champs Elysées

Designed by Le Nôtre, it has an array of beautiful flowerbeds and fountains; several of the surrounding buildings, such as the Théâtre Renaud-Barrault, date from the 19th century (its restaurant would provide a pleasant break at this point).
Continue up the Champs Elysées.

7 Rond-Point to the Arc de Triomphe

This section offers a marked contrast with the more pastoral lower section. Of the fashionable mansions built around 1860, only one has survived, No. 25. It belonged to La Païva, an adventuress whose receptions were attended by writers and artists. The wide pavements are continually teeming with a colourful cosmopolitan crowd attracted by the shopping arcades, cafés, restaurants, cinemas, and big stores like Virgin Megastore. On the quieter, south side is Fouquet's Restaurant, where celebrities come to be seen.

Nearby

Jardin des Tuileries, Musée de l'Orangerie, Madeleine, Musée Jacquemart-André, Avenue Montaigne, Palais de Tokyo, Musée Guimet, Théâtre des Champs Elysées.

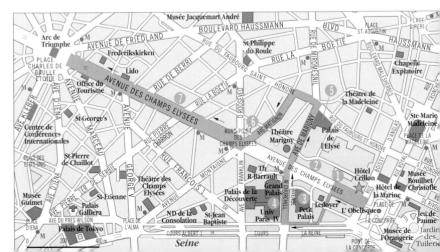

Bastille

Even though all traces of the gruesome past disappeared long ago, the name Bastille is still charged with significance. In the minds of French people it has remained a symbol of the fight for freedom, commemorated every year on 14 July.

Street café, Place de la Bastille

The Bastille Fortress

Built in the 14th century as part of new fortifications to extend the city on the Right Bank, it was also intended as a residence for Charles V, who felt safe here. During the reign of Louis XIII it became the hated state prison and symbol of oppression.

The Bastille held some famous prisoners, including the Man in the Iron Mask, presumed to be Louis XIV's twin brother, the finance minister, Fouquet, and the philosopher, Voltaire. Shortly before the Revolution the prison was partially cleared and held only seven prisoners when the mob took it by storm on 14 July 1789. However, its fall unleashed the spirit of freedom throughout France.

Demolition began soon after. Some of the stones were used for the construction of the Pont de la Concorde, and within a year there was no trace of the massive fortress. On the first anniversary of the fall of the Bastille, people danced on the site.

The Place de la Bastille

The central column, called the Colonne de Juillet (July Column), commemorates the Parisians who died during the July 1830 Revolution. This lasted only three days, *les Trois Glorieuses;* the victims were buried underneath the monument, and their names carved on the shaft. At the top of the 50-m high column stands the elf-like figure of the *Génie de la Liberté*, the Spirit of Liberty. Paving stones follow the outline of the Bastille fortress on this otherwise ordinary square, which has become a traditional meeting place for demonstrations and celebrations.

The Opéra Bastille

In 1989, the fate of the whole district took a different turn with the opening of Paris's second opera house, which had already become a controversial issue in various Parisian circles. It was intended to be technically more modern, and created a new artistic centre in the less favoured eastern part of Paris. The Opéra Bastille, built by the young Canadian architect, Carlos Ott, was inaugurated on 13 July 1989, as a preamble to the celebrations for the bicentenary of the French Revolution.

In stark contrast to the ornate Opéra Garnier, the gently curved, sober façade of the building catches the faintest ray of sunlight, thus brightening up the surrounding area.

Tel: 08 36 69 78 68 for guided tours.

www.opera-de-paris.fr
Admission charge. Métro: Bastille.

The Bastille District

Traditionally occupied by craftsmen and small shopkeepers, the district had, by the end of the 1970s, become generally run-down. Following complete renovation, it shows every sign of becoming as chic and sought after a place as its neighbour, the Marais. Art galleries, bars, and fashionable nightclubs are to be found cheek by jowl with old-fashioned shops and dilapidated houses. The most colourful and liveliest streets are the rue de la Roquette and the rue de Lappe to the north of the square.

The Pavillon de l'Arsenal

Between the place de la Bastille and the Seine is the Port de Plaisance de Paris Arsenal, a new marina. To the southwest, at the end of the boulevard Henri IV, a museum, the Pavillon de l'Arsenal, illustrates architecture and town planning in Paris through the ages and new developments through changing temporary exhibitions.
21 boulevard Morland, 75004. Tel: 01 42 76 33 97. www.pavillon-arsenal.com
Open: weekdays 10.30am–6.30pm, Sun 11am–7pm. Closed: Mon.
Métro: Sully-Morland.

Nearby
The Marais, and Ile St-Louis.

Place de la Bastille: a bustling crossroads where a prison once stood

Ever since Paris was granted independent status in the 13th century, Parisians have never hesitated to rise against excessive political power and the city has come to be considered as a very sensitive barometer of discontent.

The first major duel between the monarchy and the French people was fought and won in Paris in 1789. The signal was given when the crowd swept along the Faubourg St-Antoine to bring down the mighty Bastille on 14 July (still celebrated as a national holiday today). As a symbolic gesture, the Pont de la Concorde was later completed with stones from the hated prison, so that 'the people could forever trample the ruins of the old fortress'. Time and again, Parisians took the initiative, marching on Versailles to ask the king for bread, charging the Tuileries guards, listening to their leaders' fiery speeches in the Palais-Royal gardens, watching with gruesome curiosity as the rickety carts full of condemned prisoners jolted along the streets to the place of execution, or simply dancing and rejoicing on the Champ de Mars on the first anniversary of Bastille Day.

Scenes like these are vividly described in Dickens' *Tale of Two Cities*. King Louis XVII was executed by guillotine in the place de la Concorde (then the place de la Révolution) on 21 January 1793.

During the 19th century, the streets of Paris were set ablaze on several occasions by fierce fighting across hurriedly erected barricades. With the 1848 uprising, which began in the boulevard des Capucines, Paris did away with the monarchy for good. Yet in 1871, the Commune of Paris again challenged the government in a contest that ended in bloodshed in the Père-Lachaise cemetery. This time the Parisians lost.

A hundred years later, they showed that tradition could easily be revived when, in May 1968, students and workers barricaded the streets, bringing about General de Gaulle's resignation.

Left: the storming of the Bastille; facing page: Louis XVI as prisoner

Paris

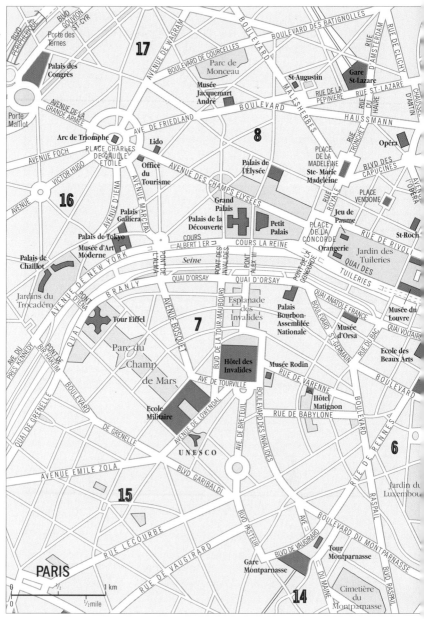

PARIS

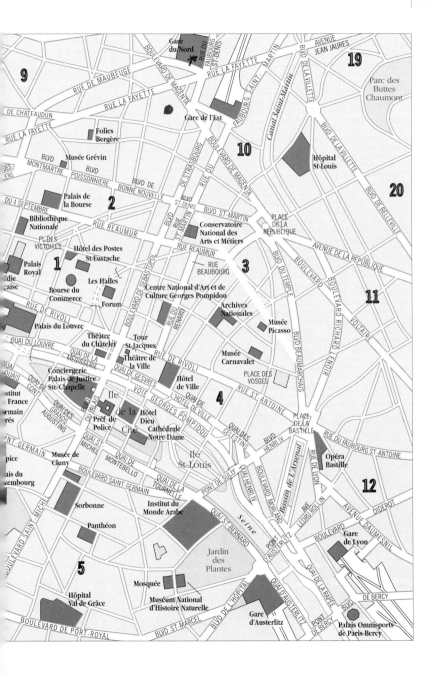

9

Gare
du Nord

RUE DE MAUBEUGE

RUE LA FAYETTE

BOULEVARD DE MAGENTA

RUE DU FAUBOURG ST-DENIS

AVENUE
JEAN JAURES

BLVD DE LA VILLETTE

19

E DE CHATEAUDUN

RUE LA FAYETTE

RUE LA FAYETTE

Gare de l'Est

Parc des
Buttes
Chaumont

FAUBOURG SAINT- MARTIN

Canal Saint-Martin

BLVD DE LA VILLETTE

Folies
Bergère

BLVD
MONTMARTRE

Musée Grévin

BLVD
POISSONNIERE

BLVD DE
BONNE NOUVELLE

DES
IENS

10

Hôpital
St-Louis

20

BLVD DE BELLEVILLE

Palais de
la Bourse

DU 4 SEPTEMBRE

2

BLVD ST-MARTIN

DE STRASBOURG

BOULEVARD DE MAGENTA

RUE DU

Bibliothèque
Nationale

RUE REAUMUR

BLVD
ST-DENIS

BLVD
ST-MARTIN

Conservatoire
National des
Arts et Métiers

PLACE
DE LA
RÉPUBLIQUE

AVENUE DE LA RÉPUBLIQUE

PL DES
VICTOIRES

Hôtel des Postes

RUE REAUMUR

Palais
Royal

édie
aise

St-Eustache

1

Les Halles

RUE
BEAUBOURG

3

BOULEVARD DE SEBASTOPOL

RUE DU TEMPLE

BOULEVARD

BOULEVARD RICHARD LENOIR

11

VOLTAIRE

Bourse du
Commerce

RUE DE RIVOLI

Forum

Centre National d'Art et de
Culture Georges Pompidou

RUE DU RENARD

Archives
Nationales

Musée
Picasso

BLVD BEAUMARCHAIS

Palais du Louvre

QUAI DU LOUVRE

Théâtre
du Châtelet

QUAI DE LA
MEGISSERIE

Tour
St-Jacques

Théâtre de
la Ville

RUE DE RIVOLI

Musée
Carnavalet

Hôtel
de Ville

PLACE DES
VOSGES

UAI
QUAIS

QUAI
CONTI

Conciergerie
Palais de Justice
Ste-Chapelle

QUAI DE GESVRES

Île
de la
Cité

VOIE GEORGES POMPIDOU

L'HOTEL DE VILLE

QUAI DE

QUAI DES
CELESTINS

RUE ST-ANTOINE

PLACE
DE LA
BASTILLE

BLVD HENRI IV

RUE DU FAUBOURG ST-ANTOINE

stitut
France
ermain
rés

QUAI DES
GRANDS
AUGUSTINS

Préf de
Police

Hôtel
Dieu

Cathédrale
Notre-Dame

Bassin de l'Arsenal

RUE DE LYON

Opéra
Bastille

12

 NT-GERMAIN

QUAI ST-
MICHEL

Musée de
Cluny

QUAI DE
MONTEBELLO

Île
St-Louis

Seine

QUAI HENRI IV

QUAI MORLAND

BOULEVARD DE L'ARSENAL

AVE
LEDRU ROLLIN

DIDEROT

AVENUE DAUMESNIL

pice

BOULEVARD SAINT-GERMAIN

Sorbonne

ais du
xembourg

QUAI DE LA
TOURNELLE

PONT DE SULLY

Institut du
Monde Arabe

QUAI ST-BERNARD

PONT
D'AUSTERLITZ

BOULEVARD

Gare
de Lyon

BOULEVARD SAINT-MICHEL

Panthéon

5

Mosquée

Jardin
des
Plantes

QUAI DE LA RAPEE

QUAI D'AUSTERLITZ

DE BERCY

Hôpital
Val-de-Grâce

Muséum National
d'Histoire Naturelle

Gare
d'Austerlitz

PONT
DE BERCY

BLVD

BOULEVARD DE PORT-ROYAL

BLVD ST-MARCEL

BLVD DE L'HOPITAL

Palais Omnisports
de Paris-Bercy

Bridges

Thirty bridges of greatly varying styles span the River Seine within the *boulevard périphérique*. Vital links between the left and right banks, they open up large vistas across the city, thus directly contributing to its unity. Although some of them may have been rebuilt several times, their names often recall customs or events from various periods of the capital's history.

Gleam of gilt on the Pont Alexandre III

The Cité Bridges
The Petit-Pont and the Pont Notre-Dame

In Roman times these were the only bridges crossing the river via the Ile-de-la-Cité. The Petit-Pont, so-called because it is the smaller of the two, was first built of stone when the construction of Notre-Dame was undertaken, but periodic floods have taken their toll, and it has been rebuilt 11 times. The present bridge dates from 1853. The Pont Notre-Dame, overladen with richly decorated houses, also had to be rebuilt several times. The present one dates from 1913.
Métro: St-Michel or Cité.

Petit-Pont, at the Seine's narrowest point

The Pont au Change

Although built between 1858–60, this bridge has a medieval name a reminder of the days when the houses and shops built on it belonged to money changers.
Métro: Châtelet.

The Pont au Double

This bridge, linking the Left Bank and the island, acquired its strange name in the Middle Ages because the toll imposed at that time was a coin named a *double*.
Métro: St-Michel.

The Pont-Neuf

Curiously enough, this is the oldest bridge in Paris, built in the 16th century. Situated at the tip of the Ile-de-la-Cité, it offers exceptional views downriver. It was never built on, a great novelty at the time, but the carvings that decorate it illustrate 'dentists' busily pulling teeth, entertainers, and assorted stalls, which were all part of the daily scene 400 years ago. The two halves, which are not in line, are separated by the place du Pont-Neuf, where there is an equestrian statue of King Henri IV. Although it has been

restored many times, the bridge remains unchanged to this day.
Métro: Pont-Neuf.

The Pont Alexandre III
Built for the 1900 Exposition Universelle, this bridge provides a link between the classical architecture of Les Invalides and the pompous steel and glass style of the Grand Palais. Each end is adorned with two allegorical sculptures, featuring medieval France and modern France on the Left Bank side, Renaissance France and France under Louis XIV on the Right Bank side.
Métro: Invalides.

The Pont de l'Alma
The original bridge built in 1854 to commemorate a Franco-British victory during the Crimean War had to be replaced 20 years ago because the supports were sinking. However, the Zouave soldier beneath it, who indicates the level of the river, was preserved and is a great favourite even today.
Métro: Alma-Marceau.

The Pont des Arts
The city's first pedestrian iron bridge is a romantic structure dating from 1803.
Métro: Pont-Neuf.

The Pont de la Concorde
Begun in 1788 by the civil engineer, Jean Rodolphe Perronnet, it was only completed after the fall of the Bastille. Since then, it has reflected many political upheavals by changing its name every time. In 1830, the name Concorde was definitely adopted.
Métro: Assemblée Nationale.

The Pont-Royal
This bridge epitomises the discreet elegance that is one of the most attractive features of Paris. It was built by Jacques Gabriel during the reign of Louis XIV – hence its royal name.
Métro: Rue du Bac.

The Pont-Neuf, with 12 varying arches

Centre Georges Pompidou

Its full name – Centre National d'Art et de Culture Georges Pompidou – gives a fair idea of the vast scope of this multi-purpose cultural centre, and explains its enormous popularity, in spite of the controversy that is still going on about its design more than 20 years after its inauguration.

Street performers draw crowds at the Centre

Beaubourg
After the removal of the old food market in 1968, the Beaubourg area was included in the huge town-planning programme centred round Les Halles. President Pompidou then decided to build a multi-purpose centre for modern and contemporary art on the site (*see* Walk *pp38–9*).

A Futuristic Design
Two young architects, Richard Rogers (British) and Renzo Piano (Italian), designed the complex, which was inaugurated in 1977, three years after President Pompidou's death. To some people it looks like an oil refinery or even scaffolding on a building site, while others, with a more optimistic outlook, see it as a contemporary piece of sculpture. In order to have as much free space as possible inside, lifts, stairs, escalators, and ventilation shafts were fitted on the outside, hence its cluttered appearance.

There is a public information library with French and foreign books, slides, and films; an industrial design centre featuring architecture, town planning, and industrial design; an acoustics and music research centre for the purpose of sound experimentation; a children's workshop; a cinema; an assortment of rooms for temporary exhibitions, concerts, and lectures; and, of course, the Musée National d'Art Moderne. *A laissez-passer d'une journée (day pass) will enable you to see all the exhibitions and to visit the museum.*

Musée National d'Art Moderne
This is situated on the third and fourth floors; the entrance is on the fourth floor, which you can reach via the serpent-like escalator accessible from the main hall.

The collections of the former Musée d'Art Moderne, retracing the evolution of art through the 20th century, were transferred from the Palais de Tokyo and have since been considerably extended to include contemporary art.

The third floor houses frequently renewed exhibits of abstract and figurative contemporary art from 1965 onwards, while the fourth floor displays all the major currents of modern art from 1905 to 1965. On this floor there are two main sections: on the south (St-Merri) side as you enter, you can see the early 20th-century trends – Fauvism and Cubism – while on the north side the main post-World War I trends are represented.

The South Side

The striking colours characteristic of Fauvism are illustrated in works by Derain, Vlaminck and, above all, Matisse, while Bonnard, whose work does not fit into the main trends, is also well represented.

There is a large selection of works by the main exponents of Cubism: Braque, Picasso, Gris, and also Léger.

The North Side

Abstract art is represented by Mondrian, Kupka, Klee, and Delaunay. The sombre, mystic style of Rouault and Chagall's world of fantasy dominate the 1920s and '30s, beside the Dada movement which deliberately derided society.

Surrealism is well represented by Dali, Magritte, Ernst, Miró, and Masson; so is the Cobra Group headed by Asger Jorn after World War II. The American school of Abstract Expressionism is strikingly represented by Pollock's 'drip-and-splash' style. The 1960s saw the advent of New Realism, and Pop Art flourished with Andy Warhol.

The fifth floor offers you a chance to relax in the pleasant cafeteria and enjoy beautiful views over the capital.

75191 Paris Cedex 04.
Tel: 01 44 78 12 33. Open: daily
11am–9pm. Closed: Tue. Admission
charge. Métro: Rambuteau, Châtelet, &
Hôtel de Ville.

Pompidou Centre: something for everyone

Walk: Beaubourg and Les Halles

Major redevelopment gave this district a new lease of life in the 1970s, and today the area attracts a crowd of young trendsetters, while the gastronomic tradition has been maintained by the score of small restaurants that used to surround the old food market.

Allow 2 hours (excluding visit to Georges Pompidou Centre).

Coming out of the Hôtel de Ville métro station, follow avenue Victoria and turn right into rue St-Martin.

1 Tour St-Jacques

The Tour St-Jacques on the left is all that remains of the 16th-century church of

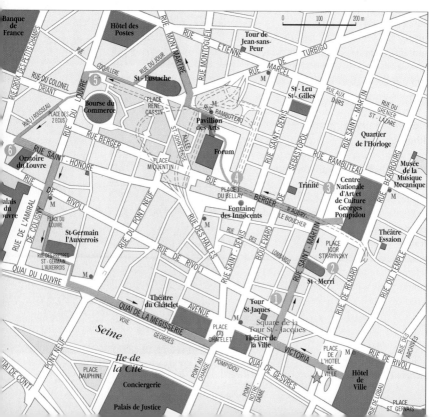

St-Jacques-de-la-Boucherie, a starting point for pilgrims bound for Santiago de Compostela. Nearby there is a statue of Pascal, who conducted barometric experiments in the tower.
Continue along rue St-Martin.

2 Around St-Merri

The names of the streets surrounding the late-Gothic church of St-Merri recall their association with medieval trades. There is rue de la Verrerie (glassmakers) alongside the church and, opposite, rue des Lombards, named after the family who set themselves up as moneylenders. The rue St-Martin is lined with shops and bistros. On the north side of the church, the intrusion of the 20th century is emphasised by the colourful fountain in the middle of the place Igor-Stravinsky.
Just north of the place is the Centre Georges Pompidou (see pp36–7).

3 Centre Pompidou

Although used to designate the Centre Pompidou, Beaubourg is the name of the old district that has come into the limelight following the success of the cultural centre. North of the Centre lies the Quartier de l'Horloge: a lively pedestrian area of narrow streets and arcades, with numerous shops and a curious modern clock, called Le Défenseur du Temps (the Defender of Time), in rue Bernard-de-Clairvaux.
Return to the place Igor-Stravinsky and turn right into the rue Aubry-le-Boucher.

4 Les Halles

Rest awhile in the square des Innocents: it has the most beautiful Renaissance fountain. The neat gardens have replaced the old food market – gone underground. Escalators lead down into the Forum, a multi-level entertainment and shopping centre *(see p54–5).*
Come up on the rue Rambuteau side and walk to the church of St-Eustache (see p40), then round it for the best views.

5 Bourse du Commerce

As you leave rue du Jour, you can see the Bourse du Commerce in front of you; it replaced the city's corn exchange in 1889. To the right is rue Coquillière, lined with restaurants, including the famous Au Pied de Cochon. Halfway down rue Jean-Jacques-Rousseau on the right is the charming Galerie Véro-Dodat with its quaint shops.
At the end of the street, turn left into rue St-Honoré.

6 Oratoire du Louvre

The 17th-century church by Le Mercier was used as the royal chapel under Louis XIII, Louis XIV, and Louis XV, who listened to the sermons of famous preachers such as Bossuet. After the revolution of 1789, it became a Protestant church.
Turn right into rue du Louvre to reach the embankment; the church of St-Germain-l'Auxerrois (see p41) offers an interesting mixture of styles. Admire the lovely view of the Conciergerie from the quai de la Mégisserie. The place du Châtelet, where you can take the métro, has an impressive fountain in the middle.

Nearby
Palais du Louvre, Théâtre de la Ville.

Churches

St-Eustache: imposing inside and out

St-Etienne-du-Mont

Begun in 1492, the church was only completed in 1626, and its originality lies in its harmonious combination of styles: the chancel and the tower are late Gothic, and the Renaissance façade is unique with its three superimposed pediments. Inside, the church is well lit by a row of windows replacing the traditional triforium. The magnificent rood screen, framed by two graceful open spiral staircases, was built at the beginning of the 16th century by Antoine Beaucorps according to drawings by Philibert Delorme. Notice also the beautiful pulpit, dating from 1650, and some attractive 16th-century stained glass behind it. Further along, past the rood screen on the right, is St Geneviève's shrine, containing relics of the patron saint of Paris. The philosopher and mathematician, Pascal, and the playwright, Racine, are buried behind the chancel.

Place Ste-Geneviève, 75005, next to the Panthéon. Closed: Mon in Jul & Aug. Métro: Cardinal-Lemoine.

St-Eustache

This was the parish church of Les Halles, and now that the old food market has gone, it can be seen from afar. In 1532 work started on an imposing Gothic building modelled on Notre-Dame and dedicated to St Eustace. Although it took over 100 years to build, the original plans were followed to the letter, and it was a truly Gothic church that was consecrated in 1637. Unfortunately, the 18th-century Neo-Classical façade that replaced the original one has rather spoilt the overall effect. Many famous people are connected with St-Eustache: Richelieu and Molière were baptised within its walls; the latter was also buried there, as were the author, La Fontaine, Colbert, Louis XIV's finance minister, and the composer, Rameau. The dimensions of the building are even more impressive from the inside than the outside. Notice the unusual height of the double aisles, the fine vault, and the stained-glass windows in the chancel, dating from 1631 and featuring St Eustace among the apostles. The church is decorated with exceptional monuments and fine works of art, including *Les Pèlerins d'Emmaüs,* an early Rubens; it also has a strong musical tradition.

Rue du Jour, 75001, next to the Forum des Halles. Métro: Les Halles.

St-Germain des Prés

This was the church of a powerful Benedictine abbey, a great centre of learning, which owned most of the Left Bank until the 17th century. The abbey buildings were destroyed during the 1789 Revolution, but the Romanesque church was saved and restored in the 19th century. It offers an original mixture of styles: the chancel and nave are Romanesque with Gothic vaulting, the massive tower acquired a steeple in the 19th century, and the original porch is masked by a door added in 1607. Inside, the chancel and ambulatory are the most interesting parts: notice the traditional carvings on the capitals and the ornamental triforium; the marble shafts of its columns come from the original 6th-century church.
Place St-Germain-des-Prés, 75006. Métro: St-Germain-des-Prés.

St-Germain-l'Auxerrois

The church was built in the 12th century, but has been continually remodelled for 400 years. As a result, it has a Romanesque belfry, a Gothic chancel, and a late-Gothic porch, while the aisle round the chancel is Renaissance. It is unfortunately associated with one of the darkest episodes of French history. In 1572, its bells gave the signal for the Massacre of St Bartholomew when thousands of Protestants were murdered as a result of a plot between the Cardinal, Duc de Guise, Catherine de Médicis, Charles IX, and the future Henri III. Inside, there are some interesting works of art, including a 16th-century Flemish reredos in the fourth chapel on the left

of the nave, 15th-century stained glass in the transept and the rose windows, and a polychrome statue of St-Germain in front of the chancel.
Place du Louvre, 75001. Métro: Louvre.

Other Churches
Eglise du Dôme des Invalides (see p57).
La Madeleine (see pp104–5).
Notre-Dame (see pp92–3).
Notre-Dame-des-Blancs-Manteaux (see p73).
Notre-Dame-des-Victoires (see p97).
Oratoire du Louvre (see p39).
Sacré-Coeur (see p100).

Stunning window, St-Germain-l'Auxerrois

Bathed in light: St-Gervais-St-Protais

St-Gervais-St-Protais

Dedicated to two Roman officers martyred under Nero, this church offers an interesting contrast of styles: the main part is late Gothic with a three-tiered classical façade. Inside, there are beautifully carved stalls, 16th- and 17th-century stained glass, and a fine 17th-century organ.
Place St-Gervais, 75004. Closed: Mon. Métro: Hôtel de Ville.

St-Medard

This late-Gothic church was completed in the 17th century. Inside, there is a 16th-century triptych, as well as other paintings of the French school and an interesting 17th-century organ loft.
Rue Mouffetard, 75005. Closed: Mon. Métro: Censier-Daubenton.

St-Merri

This is another late-Gothic church, completed in 1612. The interior was consider-ably remodelled under Louis XV, and the only original features are the stained-glass windows in the chancel.

The composer, Camille Saint-Saëns, used to play on the 17th-century organ, and there are regular concerts in the summer.
Rue de la Verrerie, 75004. Métro: Hôtel de Ville or Les Halles.

St-Roch

A fine example of classical architecture. Its foundation stone was laid by Louis XIV in 1653, but work was delayed through lack of funds and it was not completed until the 18th century. The façade, in the Jesuit style, dates from 1735. In 1795, Bonaparte charged a group of royalist rebels. The bullet holes can still be seen on the façade.
Rue St-Honoré, 75001. Closed: Sun except between 5–6.30pm. Métro: Pyramides or Tuileries.

St-Séverin

Situated in one of the oldest districts of Paris, St-Séverin is named after a hermit who lived in the area in the 6th

---

The Butte St-Roch

The church of St-Roch was originally built on a hillock upon which stood several windmills. The butte was levelled off as part of Baron Haussmann's ambitious town-planning programme, and the windmills all disappeared, except one, the Moulin Radet. This was removed to another high position, the Butte Montmartre, where you can still see it, in rue Lepic!

century. Work on the present building began in the 13th century, and went on until 1530. Thus, the façade and part of the nave are basically early Gothic, while the rest is late Gothic. In 1681, the Grande Mademoiselle, Louis XIV's cousin, had the chancel altered by the famous architect, Le Brun. Furthermore, the 13th-century west door originally belonged to a nearby church, which was demolished in 1839. Inside, the most remarkable feature is the double ambulatory, with its spiral central columns looking like palm trees under the ribbed vaulting. There is beautiful 16th-century stained glass in the upper windows, and modern stained glass by Bazaine in the chapels at the east end.

Rue des Prêtres-St-Séverin, 75005.
Open: Mon–Fri.
Métro: St-Michel or Cluny-La Sorbonne.

St-Sulpice

The church was originally built by the Abbey of St-Germain-des-Prés as a parish church for the surrounding area. The present building was started in 1646, and many architects worked on it until 1732, when it was decided to abandon the austere classical style. The Florentine architect, Servandoni, was selected to give the church an Italian-style façade.

Notice two giant shells mounted on supports carved by Pigalle as you enter; they were offered by the Venetian Republic in 1745. The first chapel on the right as you face the chancel has remarkable murals full of romantic inspiration, painted by Delacroix between 1849 and 1861.

Place St-Sulpice, 75006, near the Luxembourg gardens and St-Germain-des-Prés. Métro: St-Sulpice.
The Musée Delacroix is nearby.

St-Julien-le-Pauvre (see p61).
St-Louis-des-Invalides (see p57).
St-Louis-en-l'Ile (see p47).
St-Nicolas-du-Chardonnet (see p62).
St-Paul-St-Louis (see p71).
St-Pierre-de-Montmartre (see p75).
St-Thomas-d'Aquin (see p103).
Ste-Chapelle (see pp100–101).

The classical façade of St-Roch

Ile-de-la-Cité

It is no coincidence that the history of Paris began on this small, boat-shaped island in the middle of the Seine. Although the river has lost its once essential role, this tiny strip of land, known as the Ile-de-la-Cité, has remained the heart of the great metropolis that developed around it.

The Conciergerie illuminated

Lutetia
This was the name given to the city by the first known settlers, the Parisii: it was a Celtic word meaning 'a dwelling surrounded by water'.

The 'Cité'
The Romans brought organisation and prosperity, but after the fall of the Roman Empire, the small island was in peril once again. Although it miraculously escaped the Huns, the Franks besieged it and eventually conquered it. When King Clovis made it his capital in 508, it became known as the 'Cité'. Its renewed prosperity attracted attention and it was soon threatened by Norman raids. The city was sacked several times until Eudes, Count of Paris, reinforced its fortifications and successfully defended it in 885. For more than 100 years afterwards, however, the town remained within the perimeter of the island.

The Role of the Cathedral
As a centre of learning, the cathedral played an essential role in maintaining the influence of the Cité after the town began to spread along the banks of the river. Schools flourished between the north side of Notre-Dame and the Seine, an area that belonged to the canons of the cathedral. Abélard was among the many students drawn to the Cité by the reputation of its teaching, and it was in the cloister school that he first met Héloïse *(see p60)*. By the end of the 13th century, there were no fewer than 22 chapels and churches in the vicinity of the cathedral.

The Supreme Court
From the 14th century onwards, the kings of France ceased to live in the Cité, preferring the Louvre and other royal residences outside Paris. The royal palace became the seat of the supreme court of justice. During the Terror, the dreaded *Tribunal révolutionnaire* held its sessions there, next door to the notorious Conciergerie.

A Quiet Revolution
Naturally, the island has changed considerably since the Middle Ages, but its most spectacular remodelling took place during the second half of the 19th century. It was during that time that the area round the cathedral was cleared and began to look as it does today.

The Palais de Justice
This part of the old royal palace, many

times destroyed by fire, and considerably extended in the 19th century, has completely lost its medieval aspect, but it is still worth walking across the main courtyard to the bustling Galerie Marchande to get the feel of the place, before visiting the Ste-Chapelle and the Conciergerie.

Ste-Chapelle, 4 boulevard du Palais, 75001. Open: 10am–5pm.

The Conciergerie

This is the oldest part of the former royal palace, bordering the Seine along the quai de l'Horloge. It gets its name from the *concierge* (caretaker) who looked after the royal residence and was allowed to levy taxes. The building already served as a prison before the Revolution, and during the Terror it held such famous prisoners as Marie Antoinette and Danton. Guided tours take you through the Salle des Gardes and the impressive Salle des Gens d'Armes with superb Gothic vaulting to the vast kitchens, the Galerie des Prisonniers, and Marie Antoinette's cell.

Conciergerie, 1 quai de l'Horloge, 75001. Tel: 01 53 73 78 50. Open: Apr–Sep 9.30am–6.30pm, Oct–Mar 10am–5pm. Admission charge.

Nearby
Ile St-Louis (*see pp46–7*); churches of St-Séverin and St-Julien-le-Pauvre; picturesque streets: place St-Michel; **Ste-Chapelle** (*see pp100–101*); **Cluny museum** (*see p61*); **Notre-Dame cathedral** (*see pp92–3*).

Ile-de-la-Cité, ancient heart of Paris

Walk: The Ile-de-la-Cité and Ile St-Louis

This is the heart of medieval Paris: the bustling Ile-de-la-Cité with Notre-Dame Cathedral solidly camped at its eastern end and, next to it, the smaller, quieter, Ile St-Louis. *Allow 2–3 hours.*

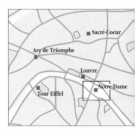

From St-Michel métro station cross the Pont St-Michel, then turn right along the quai du Marché Neuf.

1 Place du Parvis Notre-Dame

Across the vast square, created by Haussmann, stands the austere Gothic cathedral that Parisians refer to, with pride and affection, simply as Notre-Dame *(see pp92–3)*. Gallo-Roman and medieval remains are displayed in the Crypte Archéologique, beneath the Parvis. On the south side stands the statue of Charlemagne.

The incomparable cathedral of Notre-Dame

Coming out of the cathedral, turn right along the north side.

2 The Old Cloister Quarter

The rue Chanoinesse gives a fair idea of what the area looked like in the 13th century. It was here that the canons lived and taught; original houses at Nos 22 and 24 bring to mind the moving story of Héloïse and Abélard *(see p60)*.
Turn left along quai de la Corse, then left again into rue de la Cité.

3 Place Louis-Lépine

During the week, the square is the site of a colourful flower market, and on Sundays a no less picturesque but noisier bird market takes place.
Continue along rue de Lutèce. Facing are the Palais de Justice, the law courts and the Ste-Chapelle. Turn right, then left along quai de l'Horloge, past the Conciergerie, to reach place Dauphine.

4 Place Dauphine

This is a haven of peace where you can stop at one of the small restaurants and admire two of the original 17th-century brick and stone houses at Nos 12 and 14. Beyond the statue of Henri IV, the square du Vert Galant affords beautiful views of the river.

Cross over to the Left Bank, turn left and follow the embankment, lined with bookstalls, past Notre-Dame, then cross the Pont de l'Archevêché and the Pont St-Louis and turn left.

5 Quai de Bourbon

In striking contrast to the feverish activity of the Cité and the Left Bank, the Ile St-Louis offers a peaceful village atmosphere, nowhere more apparent than along the cobbled quai de Bourbon, lined with classical mansions. At the corner of rue des Deux Ponts, Au Franc Pinot, which has a restaurant in the vaulted cellars and a wine bar on the ground floor, is a pleasant place to stop. *Continue along quai d'Anjou to No. 17.*

6 Hôtel de Lauzun

Built by Le Vau in 1657, the Hôtel de Lauzun, with its gilded-dolphin waterspouts, had many famous occupants, including the poet Charles Pierre Baudelaire, who wrote much of *Les Fleurs du Mal* here, and the composer Wagner. It now belongs to the City of Paris.
Further on, turn right into rue St-Louis-en-l'Ile.

7 Rue St-Louis-en-l'Ile

This is the main street of the island. The 17th-century church of St-Louis has an unusual clock outside and a richly decorated interior. A few doors away, at No. 31, is the ice cream specialist, Berthillon.
Turn left into rue des Deux Ponts, then cross the bridge. Facing you is the famous but expensive restaurant, La Tour d'Argent, and on your left the strangely modern Institut du Monde Arabe (see p88). Turn right and follow the embankment back to place St-Michel.

Nearby
Hôtel des Monnaies, Institut du Monde Arabe, churches of St-Séverin and St-Julien-le-Pauvre, place du Châtelet, and Hôtel de Ville.

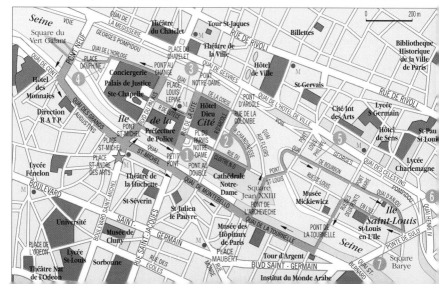

The Concorde

The place de la Concorde or la Concorde, as it is simply called, is undoubtedly the most splendid square in Paris. Its impressive size, harmonious proportions, and superbly elegant setting are the striking features of this true masterpiece of town planning. Because of its strategic position at the crossroads of the main east-west and north-south flows of traffic, it gets very congested at times.

La Madeleine overlooking the place de la Concorde

A Royal Square

The square was commissioned by the aldermen of Paris as a token of their admiration for Louis XV. Ambitious plans submitted by the architect Jacques-Ange Gabriel were approved and a vast area of over 8 hectares of drained marshland was chosen on the edge of town.

The square, which was built over a period of 20 years from 1755 to 1775, was originally surrounded by a moat and balustrade, and an equestrian statue of Louis XV by Bouchardon was placed in its centre.

Tragic Beginnings

Before work was completed, tragedy struck: in 1770, a huge crowd had gathered on the square to celebrate the wedding of Marie Antoinette and the future Louis XVI, when panic caused over 100 people to be crushed to death in the moat.

Twenty-two years later, the guillotine was set up on the square, which had been renamed place de la Révolution. In 1795, the dreaded instrument was dismantled and the square renamed place de la Concorde as a symbol of hope and peace!

Reconciliation

It was not until 1836 that the name was adopted for good. The square was partly redesigned by the architect Hittorff and the decoration completed. King Louis-Philippe decided against another statue in the centre and chose instead a neutral monument, a 3,000-year-old Egyptian obelisk.

The Obelisk

The obelisk, which comes from the temple of Luxor, was a gift from the viceroy of Egypt, Muhammad Ali. It is covered with hieroglyphs which detail the life of Rameses II, and the drawings on the base depict the process of dismantling and transporting it, and erecting it on its present site. The two large fountains are modelled on those in St Peter's Square in Rome.

The views from the centre of the square are magnificent. To the west are the Champs Elysées and the Arc de Triomphe, to the east the Jardin des Tuileries, the Arc de Triomphe du

Carrousel and the Louvre beyond, to the north the rue Royale, closed off by the Madeleine, and to the south, the Pont de la Concorde and the Assemblée Nationale across the river.

Assemblée Nationale: 128 rue de l'Université, 75007. Tel: 01 40 63 64 08. Authorised group visits only. Métro: Assemblée Nationale.

The Twin Mansions

The colonnades of the two identical buildings marking the entrance to the rue Royale were modelled on that of the Louvre. The Hôtel de la Marine is on the right as you face the Madeleine, and the Hôtel Crillon is on the left. This is now a world-famous luxury hotel, but in 1778, soon after it was built, it was the venue for the signing of an important treaty between France and the newly founded United States of America.

Statues Round the Square

To complete the decoration, eight statues representing various French towns stand in the corners of the square. Outside the Tuileries' gates are two figures on winged horses by Coysevox, representing Fame and Mercury, and, to complement them, the famous *Chevaux de Marly* by Coustou were specially brought from Louis XIV's castle to mark the entrance to the Champs Elysées. Both sets now displayed are replicas, as the marble originals have been taken to the Louvre.

Nearby

The Madeleine, Place Vendôme, Jardin des Tuileries, Musée de l'Orangerie, Musée d'Orsay, Petit Palais, and Grand Palais.

La Concorde, once far from peaceful, offers grand views of the city

FAUBOURG ST-GERMAIN

This elegant district bordering the Seine between the fashionable St-Germain-des-Prés and the stately Hôtel des Invalides, had its heyday in the 18th century. Two main thoroughfares, boulevard St-Germain and boulevard Raspail, cut across it, carrying fast-moving traffic, while the side streets, taken over by ministries, embassies and official residences, are wrapped in the kind of secluded atmosphere usually found in museums. Indeed, beautifully restored mansions of all sizes (some of them still privately owned) line the streets.

The imposing building of Les Invalides

An Aristocratic District

The name *faubourg* (suburb) is the only reminder of the area's suburban beginnings, when it was open countryside surrounding the Abbey of St-Germain des Prés. Around 1680, the aristocracy and the rich started to move in and, in the space of 50 years, the Faubourg had supplanted the Marais as the most fashionable residential district.

The Palais Bourbon

The seat of the lower house of the French Parliament (the Assemblée Nationale) consists of two 18th-century mansions: the Hôtel de Bourbon which was originally built for one of Louis XIV's illegitimate daughters, the Duchess of Bourbon, and the Hôtel de Lassay. The two were joined in 1764 and a Greek-style façade was added in the 19th century to match that of the Madeleine. On the place du Palais Bourbon, the original façade has kept its 18th-century appearance. To attend an Assemblée debate you must apply in writing.
128 rue de l'Université, 75007. Tel: 01 40 63 63 08. Authorised group visits only. Métro: Assemblée Nationale.

Grands Boulevards

These wide thoroughfares, slicing through the heart of the capital between the place de l'Opéra and the place de la Bastille, make you feel the real pace of Parisian life. Having replaced obsolete fortifications at the end of the 17th century, the boulevards became a popular place for strolling. However, a marked difference soon developed between east and west, the latter being the fashionable end! Today, it is still fascinating to notice the change as you walk east from the Opéra.

Places of Interest
Musée d'Orsay (*see pp82–3*).
Musée de la Légion d'Honneur (*see p102*).
Musée Rodin (*see p91*).

Just off the boulevard des Italiens on the right is the Opéra Comique specialising in light opera. In the boulevard Montmartre on the left is the Musée Grévin, the famous waxworks, while on either side of the boulevard are two 19th-century shopping arcades.

Further east, two 17th-century monumental gates mark the entrance to the boulevard St-Denis and the boulevard St-Martin. South of the boulevard de Bonne Nouvelle is a rather seedy district called le Sentier, a centre of the wholesale trade in fabrics and ready-made clothes.

Streets of Special Interest
The general plan of the district is very neat, with the main *hôtels* (private residences) having been built along five parallel streets.

Nearer the river is rue de Lille with the Hôtel de Seignelay at No. 80, now the Ministère du Commerce, and the Hôtel de Beauharnais, now the German Ambassador's residence. Both were built in 1714.

Next comes rue de l'Université, so-called because the land once belonged to the university, with some of the earliest mansions: No. 78, built in 1687, and No. 51, dating from 1707.

The rue St-Dominique lost a few of its 18th-century houses when the boulevard St-Germain was opened.

In rue de Grenelle, the most imposing mansion at No. 110, dating from 1778, is now occupied by the Ministère de l'Education Nationale; the beautiful Fontaine des Quatre Saisons at Nos 57–9 *(see p53)*, and the Hôtel Bouchardon next door epitomise 18th-

century elegance and refinement. The Hôtel Biron (the Musée Rodin) and the Hôtel Matignon (the office and home of the prime minister), at 77 and 57 rue de Varenne, respectively, are probably the two most beautiful mansions of the whole district.

Nearby
Les Invalides *(see pp56–7)*.
Church of St-Germain des Prés *(see p41)*.
Musée Delacroix *(see p107)*.

The beautiful Rococo Hôtel Biron, on boulevard des Invalides, houses the Musée Rodin

Fountains

Paris has many public fountains of all shapes and sizes, faithfully reflecting the architectural style of their time. Some, like the Fontaine des Quatre Saisons in the Faubourg St-Germain, were once the only means of water supply in the whole district. Others, like the Fontaine des Quatre Points Cardinaux on place St-Sulpice, were purely ornamental.

The Fontaine des Quatre Points Cardinaux

Fontaine du Châtelet
This is one of the 15 fountains that Napoleon had built in the city. Dating from 1808, it is sometimes referred to as the Fontaine de la Victoire because it commemorates the Emperor's victories in Italy and Egypt. Most often, though, it is called the Fontaine du Palmier because its column suggests a palm tree.
Place du Châtelet, 75001, near the Hôtel de Ville. Métro: Châtelet.

Fontaine Cuvier
This very ornate fountain is dedicated to Georges Cuvier, the 19th-century zoologist who founded the study of comparative anatomy. Notice the crocodile turning its head round, something crocodiles apparently cannot do!
Corner of rue Linné and rue Cuvier, 75005, near the Jardin des Plantes. Métro: Jussieu or Monge.

Fontaine des Innocents
This Renaissance fountain gets its name from the 12th-century Sts-Innocents Church demolished at the end of the 18th century. Built in 1550 at the corner of the rue St-Denis by the architect

Pierre Lescot and the sculptor Jean Goujon, it was later moved to the centre of the square and restored in 1865, when the original reliefs round the base were removed to the Louvre.
Square des Innocents, 75001, near Les Halles. Métro: Les Halles.

Fontaine Louvois
This ornamental fountain by Visconti is a typical example of the decorative style used in urban architecture during the 19th century. The statues represent four French rivers: the Seine, Loire, Saône, and Garonne.
Square Louvois, 75002, near the Bibliothèque Nationale.
Métro: Bourse.

Fontaine de Médicis
This is the most romantic fountain in Paris and one of the main attractions of the Jardin du Luxembourg. Built in 1624 by Salomon de Brosse for Marie de Médicis, Henri IV's widow, it is in the Italian style fashionable at the time.
Jardin du Luxembourg, 75006.
Métro: Odéon.
RER: Luxembourg.

Fontaine Molière

Situated at the intersection of rues de Richelieu and Molière, this fountain is dedicated to the famous 17th-century playwright who died at No. 40 rue de Richelieu. Built by Visconti in 1844, it shows the writer deeply absorbed in his thoughts.

Rue de Richelieu, 75001, near the Palais-Royal.
Métro: Palais-Royal or Pyramides.

Fontaine de l'Observatoire

This bronze fountain by Davioud dates from 1873. It depicts the different parts of the world – Europe, Asia, Africa, and America – but not Oceania, which would have spoilt the symmetry of the composition. It is also called Fontaine des Quatre Parties du Monde.

Avenue de l'Observatoire, 75006, south of the Luxembourg gardens.
RER: Port-Royal or Luxembourg.

Fontaine des Quatre Points Cardinaux

Standing in the centre of the charming place St-Sulpice, this fountain is the work of the architect Visconti. Facing the four cardinal points of the compass are the busts of four well-known men of the church who never became cardinals.

Place St-Sulpice, 75006.
Métro: St-Sulpice, Mabillon.

Fontaine des Quatre Saisons

The street is too narrow to get a good view of this beautiful 18th-century fountain by Bouchardon. In the centre, the city of Paris looks down on the rivers Seine and Marne, while on either side are figures representing the seasons.

57–9 rue de Grenelle, 75007, at the heart of the Faubourg St-Germain.
Métro: Rue du Bac.

Fontaine St-Michel

This monumental fountain was built by Davioud during the Second Empire and is typical of the ornate style in fashion at the time. It is the favourite meeting place for young Parisians.

Place St-Michel, 75005, in the Latin Quarter.
Métro: St-Michel.

The Baroque Médicis fountain

LES HALLES

This is very much an up-and-coming district, developing round the ultra-modern Forum des Halles and rapidly regaining the popularity it lost as a result of the departure of the colourful but obsolete food market that gave the area its name (*halles* means covered market). Combined with that of Beaubourg nearby, its renovation, undertaken during the 1970s, has proved a great success both socially and culturally. (*See* Walk *pp38–9.*)

Tradition Versus Modernisation

There was much controversy about the destruction of the 19th-century Pavillons Baltard housing the old market, for which Parisians suddenly discovered a deep attachment. Firmly-rooted traditions were being threatened, they felt, and would be lost forever in the pursuit of improbable benefits. However, the planners won and work went ahead.

Forum des Halles

The originality of the complex lies in the fact that there is little to be seen from the street: galleries on four levels run round a huge crater, which provides ample daylight in the central square. From there, a maze of under-

LE VENTRE DE PARIS

The 'belly of Paris' was the evocative name given to the area in the 19th century by the novelist Emile Zola. At that time, it had been the main food supply centre of the city for centuries, growing until it reached bursting point. The Pavillons Baltard, built between 1854 and 1866, gave the market a new lease of life. However, 100 years later, the market area became congested again, and the 'belly' of Paris moved out of town to Rungis.

A popular commercial and cultural complex, Les Halles

ground 'streets', lined with shops, snack bars, and restaurants, and with direct access to the métro, covers an area of 7 hectares; large maps are available on each level to direct you to the shops of your choice *(see p39)*. There are two museums on level 1: the **Nouveau Musée Grévin**, an annexe of the waxworks in the boulevard Montmartre, depicting Paris at the turn of the century; and the **Musée Français de l'Holographie**.

In the newest part of the complex, beyond the place Carrée on level 3, a cultural and commercial area includes an auditorium and a video library, as well as sports facilities and a glass swimming pool.

Old Streets

At ground level, round the gardens, which offer a pleasant contrast to the feverish underground activity, the old streets have preserved the character of the former market district, and many of the food shops, cafés, and restaurants are still there.

Forum des Halles, 75001. Métro: Les Halles. Nouveau Musée Grévin: level 1. Tel: 01 40 26 28 50. Open: weekdays 10.30am–6.45pm, Sun 1–6.30pm. Admission charge.
Musée Français de l'Holographie: level 1. Tel: 01 40 39 96 83. Open: 10am–7pm, Sun 1–7pm. Admission charge.

Hôtel de Ville

Although the present building is fairly recent, the site has always played an essential role in the history of the capital. In the Middle Ages, the square in front of the town hall was called the

Hôtel de Ville

place de Grève because it sloped down to the river (*grève* means shore). Throughout the Ancien Régime, the site was used for public executions. In 1871, during the Commune uprising, the original town hall was destroyed by fire at the same time as the Tuileries palace.

The present building, in Neo-Renaissance style, dates from 1882. Its decoration is very elaborate, as was the fashion at the turn of the 20th century: numerous statues adorn the façade, and inside, at the top of a splendid staircase, there are reception rooms with beautiful crystal chandeliers and paintings.

4 place de l'Hôtel de Ville 75004. Tel: 01 42 76 50 49. www.paris-France.org Free guided tours by appointment only (Mon–Fri). Entrance by the north door. Métro: Hôtel de Ville.

Les Invalides

This imposing group of buildings is an outstanding example of 17th-century classical architecture, situated at the end of a vast oblong open space stretching across from the Seine. Like Versailles, it epitomises the strength and confidence of the French monarchy under Louis XIV. Moreover, the whole surrounding area, with its wide, tree-lined avenues, the Faubourg St-Germain on one side and the Champ de Mars on the other, adds to the impression of space and grandeur. Sought after by wealthy Parisians, it has become a quiet, secluded residential district.

NAPOLEON'S TOMB

In 1861, the architect Visconti designed a dramatic setting for the Emperor's tomb. In the centre of an open crypt the red porphyry sarcophagus was placed on a base of green granite from the Vosges. Visitors can view it from the encircling balustrade.

A Pensioner's Home

At the beginning of his reign, Louis XIV had difficulty in establishing himself on the throne of France, and realised the importance of a strong army. However, because of the appalling conditions faced by wounded soldiers, recruitment was difficult. In order to encourage potential recruits the king decided, in 1670, to found a hospital and pension home for 4,000 invalid ex-soldiers. Work started in 1671 and lasted for five years.

A Shining Monument

The king then commissioned the young architect Jules Hardouin-Mansart to design a church with a magnificent gilt dome. In 1840, after years of negotiation with the British government, Napoleon's remains were returned to France and officially buried in the Eglise du Dôme, and Les Invalides became a symbol of the emperor's glory.

The Esplanade des Invalides

The best way to approach the Invalides is from the Pont Alexandre III (*see p35*). The vast esplanade, designed by Robert de Cotte at the beginning of the 18th century, is 500m long and 250m wide. From here you can enjoy sweeping views of the harmonious ensemble of buildings. A formal garden, surrounded by a dry moat, has 17th- and 18th-century bronze heavy guns; beyond it,

The Dôme church with its gilded cupola

the impressive doorway, flanked by twin pavilions, is adorned by an equestrian statue of Louis XIV, dating from 1815.

The Cour d'Honneur

The paved courtyard is lined with arcades on two storeys. Four pavilions have dormer windows adorned with trophies, and in the four corners, at roof level, there are carved horses trampling the emblems of war. More heavy guns complete this imposing setting. On either side of the courtyard are the collections of the **Musée de l'Armée** (*see* Museums, *p84*), while, at the end, is the entrance to St-Louis church.

St-Louis-des-Invalides

This is the original church by Libéral Bruant, also known as the soldiers' church, a cold building decorated only with flags and standards taken from the enemy. The Eglise du Dôme is visible through a glass panel behind the altar. The magnificent organ was used for the premiere of Berlioz's *Requiem* in 1837. *Open: 10am–5pm, 6pm in summer.*

Eglise du Dôme

The Eglise du Dôme was built between 1677 and 1735. The tiered façade with Doric and Corinthian columns is adorned with statues of St-Louis, Charlemagne, and the four virtues, and enhanced by the well-proportioned dome. The interior is magnificently decorated with different marbles, painted cupolas, columns, and low reliefs. In the side chapels are the tombs of several of Napoleon's generals as well as those of Turenne, Lyautey, and Foch.

Hôtel des Invalides, 75007.
Eglise du Dôme and Musée de l'Armée;
tel: 01 44 42 37 72. Open: 10am–5pm,
6pm in summer. Admission charge.
Métro: Invalides, Latour-Maubourg, or
Varenne.

Nearby
Palais Bourbon, **Faubourg St-Germain** (*see p50*); **Champ de Mars** (*see p58*); **Tour Eiffel** (*see pp110–11*); **Pont Alexandre III** (*see p35*); **Musée Rodin** (*see p91*).

Les Invalides still houses old veterans

Walk: From the Trocadéro to the Invalides

This is the Paris of grand vistas and wide open spaces, where various architectural styles help to create an impressive setting for the most famous of the city's monuments, the Eiffel Tower.

Allow 2 to 3 hours (excluding museum visits and a climb to the top of the Eiffel Tower).

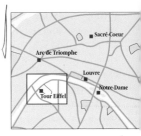

Begin from the Trocadéro métro station.

1 Place du Trocadéro

From the top of the Chaillot hill, the rather dull place du Trocadéro offers stunning views of the Left Bank. Several wide avenues radiating from it give the impression of a busy roundabout where no one cares to stop. Behind a high wall to the west is the Passy cemetery and, facing the river, the Palais de Chaillot, built for the 1937 Exposition Universelle. The name Trocadéro commemorates the capture in 1823 of Fort Trocadéro in Spain.

Pass between the curved wings of the Palais de Chaillot.

2 Jardins du Trocadéro

Stairs lead down to the gardens on either side of a long pool adorned with stone and gilt bronze statues and attractive floodlit fountains, which provide one of the most spectacular summer night shows of the capital.

Cross the Pont d'Iéna, named to commemorate Napoleon's victory over the Prussians in 1806. The bridge provides a good close-up view of the Eiffel Tower.

3 Champ de Mars

If, after the thrill of climbing up to the third floor of the Eiffel Tower, you feel the need to relax in a down-to-earth restaurant, then La Fontaine de Mars, 129 rue St-Dominique, is just what you are looking for. The vast open space, stretching from the Eiffel Tower to the Ecole Militaire, was originally designed in the 18th century as a parade ground for the nearby military academy, hence its name. Later on, it became the tradition to use it for large-scale public festivals and World Exhibitions; in 1989, almost half a million people attended the mammoth celebrations for the 100th birthday of the Eiffel Tower.

Walk across the park and turn right into avenue de la Motte Picquet.

4 Ecole Militaire

The building of this magnificent Neo-Classical military academy, designed by Louis XV's architect, Jacques-Ange Gabriel, was actually financed by a special tax on playing cards. Napoleon Bonaparte was undoubtedly its most famous cadet, passing out as a lieutenant in the

artillery with the comment: 'Will go far, given favourable circumstances'. The school is still used as an instruction centre and is closed to the public.
As you walk round the building, you might enjoy a short detour to the antique shops of the Village Suisse across the avenue de Suffren.

5 UNESCO Building
Inaugurated in 1958, this building is the result of three international architects – an American, an Italian, and a Frenchman – working together on the project, while the decoration was left to famous artists: Henry Moore (monumental sculpture), Alexander Calder (mobile), Pablo Picasso (mural), Joan Miró (ceramics), Lurçat and Le Corbusier (tapestries), and Isamu Noguchi (fountain).
Follow avenue de Lowendal and walk to

No. 51 bis, boulevard de la Tour Maubourg.

6 Musée de L'Ordre de la Libération
The order, created by General de Gaulle in 1940, is the highest honour bestowed by France in recognition of outstanding services rendered during World War II. Among the allied leaders honoured are: King George VI, Winston Churchill, and General Eisenhower.
Tel: 01 47 05 35 15 Open: 10am–5pm. Closed: Sun.
Retrace your steps and turn left. Go through the Hôtel des Invalides (see pp56–7), and walk across the Esplanade to the Invalides métro station.

Nearby
Left Bank: Village Suisse antique shops.
Musée Rodin (see p91).

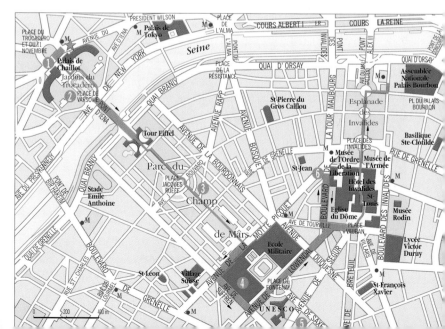

Latin Quarter

This is one of the oldest districts of Paris, rich in traditions going back to the Middle Ages, yet teeming with new ideas launched by its lively young population. Situated on the Left Bank, opposite the Ile-de-la-Cité, the district spreads from the place St-Michel uphill to the Montagne Ste-Geneviève dominated by the Panthéon and the Sorbonne. A free and easy atmosphere pervades the whole area.

The Gallo-Roman City

Roman public buildings were concentrated on the Left Bank, just across the river from the Ile-de-la-Cité occupied by the Celts. Ruins of public baths were discovered next to the Hôtel de Cluny, and those of an amphitheatre in the vicinity of the Jardin des Plantes. At the end of the 3rd century, hordes of barbarians burned down the whole Left Bank, halting development there for a long time.

A Universal Language

In the 12th century, several teachers and students broke away from the

Faculty building at the Sorbonne

HÉLOÏSE AND ABÉLARD

A tragic love story unites the names of Canon Fulbert's niece Héloïse and a young teacher from Brittany called Abélard. About 100 years before the foundation of the Sorbonne, Abélard became Héloïse's tutor at her uncle's request. They fell in love, eloped, got married, and had a son. When they returned to Paris, Canon Fulbert decided to punish Abélard by having him castrated. Abélard became a monk and a famous teacher while Héloïse took the veil, but their love survived and they went on writing passionate letters to each other.

They were buried in the same grave inside the monastery that Abélard had founded, and of which Héloïse had subsequently become the abbess. Their remains were transferred to the cimetière du Père Lachaise.

cathedral schools of the Ile-de-la-Cité and established themselves on the Left Bank. Their action soon led to the foundation of the university of Paris in 1215. Before the end of the 13th century, there were several colleges on the Montagne Ste-Geneviève welcoming students from the French provinces and other parts of Europe. These early Europeans spoke Latin, a practice which lasted until 1789.

The Sorbonne

This was the first and most successful of the many colleges that flourished in pre-revolutionary Paris. From very humble beginnings in 1253, it developed into a reputed centre of theological studies and became the seat of the powerful university. Its prestige and popularity have survived to this day. The 17th-century buildings were extensively remodelled and enlarged at the end of the 19th century. The Sorbonne church, which is open only on special occasions, dates from the beginning of the 17th century. It contains the white marble tomb of Cardinal Richelieu.

Sorbonne: for free guided tour apply in writing to M René Blanchet, Rectorat de Paris, 45 rue des Ecoles, 75005.

St-Julien-le-Pauvre

There has been a church on this site since the 6th century, as it was on the route followed by pilgrims on their way to Santiago de Compostela. The present building, dating from the late-12th century, was the university church from the 13th to the 16th century. St-Julien is now a Greek Orthodox church. Its style is transitional, partly Romanesque and

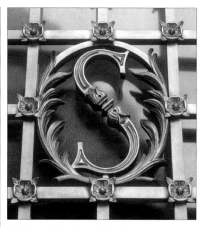

Architectural detail at the Sorbonne

partly Gothic, with a 17th-century façade.

St-Julien-le-Pauvre, rue St-Julien, 75005. Métro: St-Michel.

Hôtel de Cluny

This is one of the best examples of domestic medieval architecture. It was built in the 15th century for the abbots of the famous Cluny Abbey on the site of the ruined Roman baths. The style of the house is inspired by the Renaissance, best observed from the main courtyard. The central building has high windows and an elaborate balustrade with impressive gargoyles, while the main staircase winds up a pentagonal tower. Inside, the Musée National du Moyen Age covers all aspects of medieval art *(see p86).*

6 place Paul-Painlevé, 75005.
Tel: 01 53 73 78 16.
Open: 9.15am–5.45pm. Closed: Tue. Admission charge.
Métro: Cluny-La Sorbonne.

Walk: The Latin Quarter

This is the centre of university life, where tiny restaurants along the side streets and cafés on the boulevard St-Michel are packed at all hours.

Allow 2 hours (excluding a visit to the Musée National du Moyen Age – Thermes de Cluny).

Start from the place St-Michel, where the impressive 1860 fountain is a favourite meeting point. Take the rue de la Huchette, rue de la Harpe and rue St-Séverin to reach the church of St-Séverin (see pp42–3).

1 St-Séverin Quarter

The narrow streets and alleyways have kept their picturesque medieval names, such as 'rue de la Parcheminerie' (Parchment Street). Unfortunately, the authenticity of the district is threatened by the increasing number of cheap Greek and North African restaurants, with a welcome exception: La Cochonaille. Le Caveau de la Huchette (rue de la Huchette) is a well-known jazz cellar.

Go round the back of St-Séverin, down the rue St-Jacques to the church of St-Julien-le-Pauvre and the square Viviani. Then follow the rue Galande and the rue Lagrange to the place Maubert.

2 Place Maubert

Maubert is probably a contraction of Maître Albert, the famous 13th-century teacher. At one time the hideout of thieves and cut-throats, the area has been renovated, regaining its Left Bank atmosphere. The tiny rue Maître-Albert leads down to the river from where you get a beautiful view of Notre-Dame.

Rue de Bièvre brings you back to place Maubert.

3 St-Nicolas-du-Chardonnet

Situated a little way up the rue Monge, this unusual 17th-century church with a 20th-century façade is decorated inside with paintings by Camille Corot and Charles Le Brun, and elaborate funeral monuments.

Proceed along rue du Sommerard to Cluny House (see p86), walk up rue de la Sorbonne, past the university buildings, then left into rue Soufflot.

4 Place du Panthéon

Facing you is the vast domed Panthéon *(see p98)*, dominating the whole Latin Quarter. You can sit at one of the cafés and admire the view before going round to the left, past the bibliothèque Ste-Geneviève, famous for its ancient manuscripts.

Pass between the Panthéon and the highly original church of St-Etienne-du-Mont (see p40) and turn right into rue Clotilde, then left into rue de l'Estrapade.

5 Place de la Contrescarpe

This tiny square has been famous since the Middle Ages for its *cabaret de la*

Pomme de Pin (at No. 1), described by the famous author, François Rabelais. There is a choice of interesting cafés and restaurants here.
Following rue Lacépède to the end, you will arrive at the Fontaine Cuvier (see p52). Turn left into rue Monge.

6 Arènes de Lutèce

Rue des Arènes, on the right, leads to the ruins of a Roman theatre, discovered during the remodelling of medieval Paris in the 19th century, and now part of a public garden.
Turn left at the crossroads, right into rue Descartes, then bear left down rue de l'Ecole Polytechnique.

7 Collège de France

Since its foundation by François I in 1530, the college has maintained a tradition of independent teaching, and gives free public lectures on a wide range of subjects.
Continue along rue des Ecoles past square Paul-Painlevé. Cross boulevard St-Michel.

8 Rue Hautefeuille

This old, picturesque street on your right, by the former Ecole de Médecine, takes you back to place St-André-des-Arts (*see* rue St-André-des-Arts, *p109*).

Nearby
Jardin du Luxembourg, Jardin des Plantes.

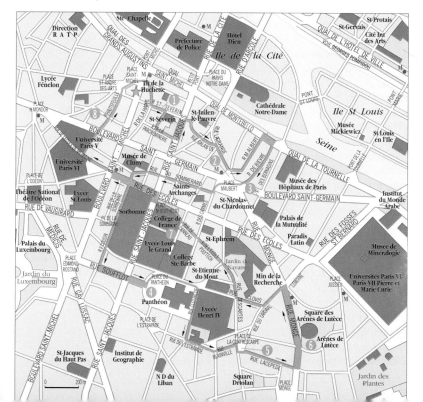

Louvre

Situated on the Right Bank, within a stone's throw of the Ile-de-la-Cité, the Louvre expanded according to the whim of successive French monarchs, and today it is one of the world's largest royal palaces. It is better known, however, for the great museum within its walls. The Grand Louvre project was designed to modernise and smarten it up, and the eye-catching glass pyramid erected in the open courtyard has renewed interest in the building's 'threatened' architectural beauty.

Interior of the Pyramide du Louvre

The Louvre Palace
The original castle was consistently extended westwards, away from the congested part of the city.

The Medieval Fortress
Built by King Philippe-Auguste at the end of the 12th century, the Louvre castle was just a massive keep surrounded by a wall and towers, designed as part of the city's fortifications. It became a royal residence when Charles V extended the city further west and protected it with new fortifications. Remains of this fortress were discovered under the Cour Carrée, and have been excavated recently as part of the Grand Louvre scheme (access through the museum).

The Renaissance Palace
Until the 16th century, the Louvre was neglected in favour of less austere residences in the Marais or on the Loire; then Francis I had part of the obsolete fortress razed, and in 1546 he commissioned Pierre Lescot to build a

new palace. Lescot worked on it until his death in 1571, entrusting the decoration to the sculptor Jean Goujon.

The Tuileries
Catherine de Médicis, Henri II's widow, initiated the extension of the Louvre westwards. She commissioned Philibert Delorme to build a new palace close to the Louvre, known as the Tuileries. Superstition prevented the queen from settling in here – an astrologer told her she would die there! In 1871 it was burned down and had to be demolished.

The Galerie du Bord de l'Eau
Catherine de Médicis had originally intended to link the two palaces by way of a long wing parallel to the river, but these plans were abandoned until Henri IV's accession to the throne. He completed the link in 1608 by having the Galerie du Bord de l'Eau and the Pavillon de Flore built.

The Cour Carrée
Louis XIII and Louis XIV concentrated

their efforts on the Cour Carrée. In 1624, the architect Lemercier built the Pavillon de l'Horloge in the centre of the west wing, which he extended by another building faithfully matching that of Pierre Lescot. The other three sides were completed by Louis XIV's architects: Le Vau, Le Brun, and Perrault, who also rebuilt the Apollo wing linking the Cour Carrée to the Galerie du Bord de l'Eau. The impressive Colonnade marks the formal entrance to the palace.

Squatters in the Louvre

Abandoned in favour of Versailles at the end of the 17th century, the palace was neglected and taken over by artists and their families; eventually, an assortment of buildings concealed the beautiful façades which were threatened with dilapidation. However, in 1793, the Galerie du Bord de l'Eau was turned into a museum.

The Carrousel

Napoleon settled in the Tuileries and restored order to the architectural jumble; he also commissioned Percier and Fontaine to build the Arc de Triomphe du Carrousel and a north wing along the rue de Rivoli, which was completed by Napoleon III.

The Grand Louvre

The purpose of this project, which began in 1981, was to create more room for the museum by refurbishing the north wing, the Richelieu wing, formerly occupied by the Ministère des Finances, and to provide badly needed public facilities. The well-known

American architect, IM Pei, consequently designed a vast new underground entrance hall over which stands a glass pyramid. The project was completed in 1999.

Palais du Louvre, 75001. For opening times, see p67. Métro: Palais-Royal.

Nearby
Jardin des Tuileries, Louvre des Antiquaires, Oratoire du Louvre, Churches of St-Roch and St-Germain-l'Auxerrois, Pont des Arts, Musée d'Orsay.

Countless masterpieces are on view in the vast halls of the Louvre

The Louvre Museum

Francis I started the royal collection in the 16th century by acquiring 12 paintings by Italian masters, which included Leonardo da Vinci's *Mona Lisa*, still the most famous of the museum's art treasures. During the reign of Louis XIV, the king's minister, Colbert, practised a policy of systematic buying, and the collection swelled to more than 2,000 paintings.

One of the many treasures in the sculpture gallery

Meanwhile, the Académie Royale de Peinture et de Sculpture, founded in 1648, was already holding its annual exhibition in the Louvre and artists were granted lodgings in the palace. Shortly after the creation of the museum in 1793, works of art were brought back from Versailles, and later Napoleon and his successors continued to enrich the collections with Greek, Assyrian, and Egyptian antiquities.

The Carrousel du Louvre
In order to avoid unnecessary delays, use the direct access from the Palais-Royal métro station to the museum through the new Carrousel du Louvre, a vast underground architectural complex which forms part of the Grand Louvre project and links the Jardin des Tuileries to the Louvre. It includes the Galerie du Carrousel, a wide alleyway lit at one end by an inverted glass pyramid and leading to the museum's entrance hall.

The Museum Today
The Louvre consists of three wings, Sully, Denon, and Richelieu, which house the museum's seven departments indentifiable by a colour code. The collections are displayed on four levels, each divided into 10 *arrondissements* accessible by means of escalators from the underground reception area, where leaflets in English, including ground plans, are available to help you decide what you want to see. There are also maps and signposts throughout the museum. If you are looking for a particular work, ask a member of staff to direct you in case there has been a rearrangement of exhibits.

The Medieval Moat
The Sully escalator leads directly to rooms depicting the history of the palace and surrounding area; from there you can go to the Sully region, or walk round the moat of the medieval fortress buried under the Cour Carrée. Objects found during the excavations include Charles VI's gilt helmet (14th-century).

Oriental Antiquities
This department houses archaeological finds from the valleys of the Euphrates and the Tigris, concerning mainly the Sumerian and Babylonian civilisations, the Elamite and Persian civilisations, the Phoenicians, and the Assyrians.

Egyptian Antiquities

The great Sphinx in pink granite makes a most impressive introduction to Egyptian art, while the Seated Scribe, dating from around 2500 BC, and the bust of Amenophis IV from Karnak are strikingly realistic masterpieces.

Greek, Etruscan, and Roman Antiquities

You cannot visit the Louvre Museum without seeing the 2nd century BC *Venus de Milo*, generally acknowledged as a perfect example of feminine beauty.

Paintings

Several paintings by Leonardo da Vinci, Titian, and Raphael are among the most outstanding works of the Italian school. Flemish and Dutch painters include Rembrandt and Van Dyck. There is also a superbly dramatic *Christ en croix* by El Greco. The French school is strongly represented by de la Tour, Poussin, Watteau, Delacroix, and Géricault.

Sculpture

Of special interest are *Les Nymphes* by Jean Goujon, *Les Chevaux de Marly* by Guillaume Coustou, a copy of which guards the entrance to the Champs Elysées, several busts by Houdon, and the *Esclaves* by Michelangelo.

Objets d'Art

The Crown Jewels, including the Regent, a 140-carat diamond, are usually the biggest attraction here. Among a wealth of other fine pieces are the Maximilian tapestries and excellent furniture by Boulle.

Musée du Louvre, Palais du Louvre, 75001, Paris Cedex 01. Tel: 01 40 20 51 51. www.louvre.fr Open: 9am–6pm, Wed to 9.45pm. Closed: Tue. Admission charge. Facilities: bookshop, audio guides, auditorium, restaurant and cafeteria which remain open after closing time. Main entrance under the glass pyramid in the Cour Napoléon. Métro: Palais-Royal.

The Louvre's vast collection of art includes many acknowledged masterpieces

Today, foreigners account for one-sixth of the capital's population; thus, over the last few decades, the character of certain areas has drastically changed. Some minorities, such as the White Russians, are fully assimilated, even if they still get together on occasions. Others, however, live in enclaves that, over the years, have acquired a strong cultural identity.

The Jewish district is situated at the heart of the Marais, within a small quadrangle formed by rue de Rivoli, rue des Francs Bourgeois, rue Vieille-du-Temple, and rue de Sévigné. There has been a Jewish community in this area since the Middle Ages, but the arrival in 1962 of a great number of Algerian Jews suddenly altered the east European flavour of the district. The rue des Rosiers is very picturesque, with its delicatessens, restaurants, felafel snack bars, and old food shops turned into fashion boutiques.

During the 1960s, tower block flats mushroomed in the 13th *arrondissement* and, as a result, a large number of Asian immigrants, the majority of them Chinese, settled in the area surrounding the porte de Choisy. As a result, the avenue d'Ivry is particularly lively with its cinemas, restaurants, supermarkets, and shops that look like pagodas.

Successive waves of immigrants, this time mainly from Africa, have settled in

the Goutte-d'Or district, just east of Montmartre, and now, more than 30 different nationalities cohabit in what must truthfully be called deteriorating conditions. Redevelopment is in the air, under-standably opposed by the locals, for what will become of the colourful little shops that make a roaring trade selling exotic groceries, junk jewellery, and African fabrics, etc?

Colonial connections, refugees, and other immigrant groups are evident in the vibrant, cosmopolitan atmosphere of Paris's ethnic commercial ventures

The Marais

This is one of the most authentic districts of Paris, with a wealth of 17th-century domestic architecture. It is also a lively area, where traditions are being rediscovered, and where variety and contrasts make strolling along its picturesque streets a real pleasure.

A new lease of life for the mansions in the Marais

Against All Odds
Only 30 years ago the Marais seemed to have irretrievably sunk back into its murky beginnings! The name suggests marshy land, and this is exactly what it was until, in the 13th century, various religious communities, including the Knights Templars, turned it into arable land. At the beginning of the 17th century, Henri IV had the place Royale (now the place des Vosges) built right at the heart of the district, and the aristocracy promptly commissioned the most renowned architects to design the splendid mansions (*hôtels*) seen there today. This was the Marais' golden age! But then fashion changed and the district, deserted by the wealthy in favour of the Faubourg St-Germain, was taken over by shopkeepers and craftsmen, while the beautiful mansions gradually became dilapidated.

A New Lease of Life
In the early 1960s, the Ministre de la Culture, André Malraux, made the district a protected area and restoration work began straight away. The Marais assumed its cultural heritage while offering its inhabitants a new quality of life. Some *hôtels* were cleverly converted into flats or turned into museums, and new shopkeepers moved in and set up smart boutiques. An artistic revival followed, which is still very apparent.

Interesting Streets
It is certainly worth taking your time, and even losing your way in the side streets north of the rue des Francs Bourgeois. There are also lively streets, which you don't want to miss. Stretching from one end of the Marais to the other, the rue des Francs Bourgeois is a commercial street lined with many fine houses, boutiques, cafés, and restaurants. The rue des Archives is well known for its leather goods and jewellery. The rue Vieille-du-Temple has an assortment of restaurants, cafés, and quaint shops, and the rue des Rosiers is the picturesque main street of the Jewish Quarter. South of the wide rue St-Antoine, the area of rue St-Paul and the Village St-Paul is a must for antiques lovers.

Some Beautiful Mansions
The Hôtel Carnavalet in the rue de Sévigné is a Renaissance mansion remodelled by Mansart in the 17th century. Madame de Sévigné lived in it for 20 years and wrote many of her famous letters there. It now houses the Musée de l'Histoire de Paris.

Across rue des Francs Bourgeois is the 1584 Hôtel de Lamoignon, one of the oldest mansions in the district.

At the corner of rue des Archives and rue des Francs Bourgeois, the **Hôtel de Soubise** is an early 18th-century residence, but its corbelled turrets are a reminder of the original 14th-century manor house. Since 1808 it has been the home of the National Archives.

The Hôtel de Sens, in rue du Figuier, is one of the few remaining medieval residences – it was built in the late-15th century. Notice the turrets and the beautiful courtyards. In rue des Archives, the Hôtel Guénégaud, built in 1650, houses the **Musée de la Chasse et de la Nature**, which has a collection of arms as well as pictures by Vernet, Oudry, and Chardin, and tapestries based on the theme of hunting.

St-Paul-St-Louis

This baroque church, which was completed in 1641, was modelled on the Gesù church in Rome. The interior is well lit and richly decorated; in the transept there is a *Christ au Jardin des Oliviers* by Delacroix.

Nearby
Hôtel de Sully 62 rue St-Antoine.
Place des Vosges (*see p99*).

Museums
Musée Cognacq Jay Hotel Donon (*see p86*); **Musée de l'Histoire de France** Hôtel de Soubise, 60 rue des Francs Bourgeois (*see p87*); **Musee Picasso** Hotel Salé (*see p90*); **Musée de la Chasse et de la Nature** 60 rue des Archives. *Tel: 01 42 72 86 43*. Open: 10am–12.30pm, 1.30–5 30pm. Closed: Tue. Admission charge. Métro: Hôtel de Ville.

Rest your feet, enjoy a drink, and watch the world go by at a Marais café

Walk: The Marais

This area of great architectural wealth is a fashionable residential district enlivened by a variety of small shops and restaurants, art galleries, and craft workshops.

Allow 2 hours (excluding museum visits).

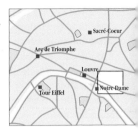

Begin from the place St-Gervais (métro Hôtel de Ville). Facing is St-Gervais-St-Protais, the oldest classical church in Paris.

1 Rue François-Miron

One of the first roads to cross the marshy area or *marais,* the street is lined with old houses of interest: Nos 11 and 13 are half-timbered, 15th-century houses; Nos 44 to 46 have splendid Gothic cellars; and further up, the 17th-century Hôtel de Beauvais (No. 68) rang with Mozart's music when the young

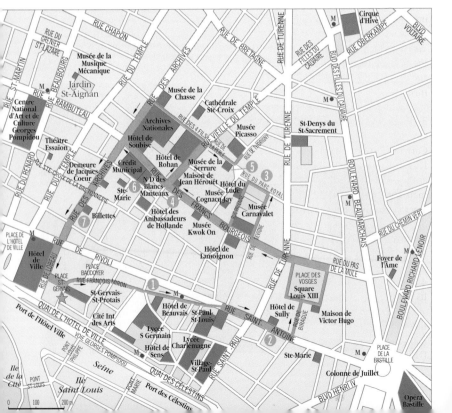

prodigy stayed there in 1763. The baroque church of St-Paul-St-Louis stands at the beginning of rue St-Antoine.

2 Rue St-Antoine

This has been the main street of the Marais since the 14th century, when it was a favourite venue for jousting contests. Henri II was fatally wounded here in 1559 in a tournament to celebrate his daughter's wedding.

The rue de Sévigné opposite the church leads to place du Marché-Ste-Catherine where you will find a good selection of restaurants. The courtyard of the 1625 Hôtel de Sully (No. 62) has impressive sculptures featuring the seasons and the elements.
Turn left into rue de Birague, leading to the place des Vosges (see pp98–9). Take rue des Francs Bourgeois going west, then turn right into rue de Sévigné.

3 Rues du Parc Royal and Payenne

On your left is the imposing Hôtel Carnavalet which houses the Musée Historique de la Ville de Paris. Turn left at the end of the street; a row of lovely mansions facing a peaceful garden make a perfect setting. In rue Payenne, opposite two elegant mansions, is another garden adorned with statues.
Turn right.

4 Rue des Francs Bourgeois

Its medieval name, referring to the almshouses built in the 14th century for the non tax-paying citizens or *francs bourgeois*, and the house of Jean Hérouët (No. 54), with its elegant turret, both recall the days when the street was the

centre of the weaving trade. Today it is lined with 17th- and 18th-century mansions, boutiques, and restaurants such as L'Orée du Marais at No. 29.
Turn right into rue Vieille-du-Temple, then right into rue de la Perle.

5 Musée de la Serrure

Housed in a smaller-scale mansion, once the home of the architect who built Les Invalides, the museum's collection traces the history of locks since Roman times.
Open: Mon 2–5pm, Tue–Fri 10am–noon, 2–5pm. Closed: weekends.

Rue de Thorigny opposite leads to the Musée Picasso (see p90). Turn back down rue de la Perle and walk along rue des 4 Fils; on the right is the Musée de la Chasse et de la Nature (see p71); turn left into rue des Archives, then left again into rue des Francs Bourgeois, past the Hôtel de Soubise.

6 Notre-Dame-des-Blancs-Manteaux

This church is famous for its woodwork, in particular its Rococo pulpit and organ loft. Concerts are given here during the Marais festival.
Return to the rue des Archives. Turn left.

7 Cloître des Billettes

Built in the 15th century as part of a monastery, this is the only medieval cloister left in Paris. The church next door is 18th-century.

Nearby
Centre Pompidou, Hôtel de Sens, Village-St-Paul, The Bastille.

Montmartre

The distinctive white outline of the Sacré-Coeur basilica, visible from almost anywhere in the city, is the universally recognised symbol of Montmartre. The name Montmartre draws on people's imaginations to keep alive the memory of its heyday. For, unlike other districts, la Butte relies entirely on its past image for survival. Quite often it looks like a vast open-air theatre where the décor never changes and the same play is enacted every day!

TOULOUSE-LAUTREC

Born into the aristocracy and crippled at an early age, Toulouse-Lautrec's sad life was made endurable by his talent and passion for painting. He portrayed scenes of Montmartre's nightlife, sketching its stars with unique realism.

A painter captures the spirit of Montmartre

The case of Montmartre is, of course, unique, for it was its picturesque rural atmosphere and its free and 'easy' life that caught the world's attention at a time when most cities were overwhelmed with industrial squalor. It had nothing to offer except its refreshing simplicity, and its artists. The artists left long ago and there only remained a few cafés and cabarets full of memories, a heritage very difficult to preserve in a rapidly changing city with a growing tourist trade.

The most interesting parts of Montmartre are today centred round rue Lepic and its market, as well as the place des Abbesses and the surrounding area. However, it is well worth strolling along rue des Saules or the place du Tertre early in the morning or out of season.

Bohemian Life
It all began in the early 19th century, when a few artists and writers wishing to lead a freer life settled on the Butte: Berlioz, Nerval, and Heine were three of the earliest residents. After the Franco-

Prussian war of 1870, Montmartre became the centre of Paris's bohemian life, inhabited by impoverished painters and poets, and visited by Parisians who flocked into the cabarets, cafés, and dance halls.

At the turn of the 20th century, the most famous of these establishments were the Chat Noir and the Moulin Rouge at the foot of the hill, the Moulin de la Galette halfway up in rue Lepic, La Bonne Franquette at the corner of rue des Saules and rue St-Rustique, and the Lapin Agile down on the other side of the hill. Artists like Renoir, Van Gogh, and Toulouse-Lautrec found their inspiration among the enthusiastic spectators and the colourful performers. They were succeeded by Utrillo, Picasso, Braque, Modigliani, and many others. This lasted until World War I, when the artists left for Montparnasse.

Musée de Montmartre

Number 12 rue Cortot is one of the oldest houses on the Butte, dating from the 17th century. The museum depicts the history of Montmartre through mementoes of its most famous inhabitants.

St-Pierre-de-Montmartre

This is one of the oldest churches in Paris, once part of the powerful Abbey of Montmartre. Built in the 12th century, it has an 18th-century façade. Inside there are some fine carvings on the Romanesque capitals, contrasting with the modern stained glass, as well as four marble columns, probably belonging to a Roman temple that stood on the site.

Montmartre, still a village at heart

Cimetière de Montmartre

Access to the cemetery is by a flight of stairs on the left of rue Caulaincourt, at the end of the bridge as you walk towards the boulevard de Clichy. Ask for a map at the entrance. Many famous artists and writers are buried here, among them the novelists Stendhal and Zola, the composer Berlioz, the poets Heine and Vigny, the painter Degas, and, more recently, the film director François Truffaut.
Rue Caulaincourt. Métro: Abbesses or Lamarck-Caulaincourt.

Nearby
Sacré-Coeur (see p100).
Musée de Montmartre 12 rue Cortot.
Tel: 01 46 06 61 11. Open: 11am–5.30pm.
Closed: Mon. Admission charge.
Espace Dali 11 rue Poulbot.
Tel: 01 42 64 40 10. Open: 10am–6.30pm
(9pm in summer). Admission charge.

Walk: Montmartre

Although it remains a symbol of bohemian life, *La Butte*,
as Parisians call it, has lost some of its romantic appeal.
There are times, however, when walking along the quaint
old streets takes you back a hundred years!
Allow 2 hours.

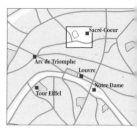

Begin from the Pigalle métro station.

1 Pigalle

For 100 years the name has been
associated with a kind of exuberant and
colourful nightlife, usually summed up
in two words: Moulin Rouge! That
famous institution is still as popular as
ever, but the area has now been taken
over by less picturesque clubs, discos,
sex shops, and pornographic cinemas. It

is not advisable for women to walk
round Pigalle at night on their own.
*Walk along boulevard de Rochechouart,
and turn left into rue de Steinkerque.*

2 Place des Abbesses

At the end of the street, a funicular leads
directly to the Sacré-Coeur Basilica.
  Turn left into rue Tardieu and
continue along the rue Yvonne-Le-Tac: a
chapel stands on the site where it is

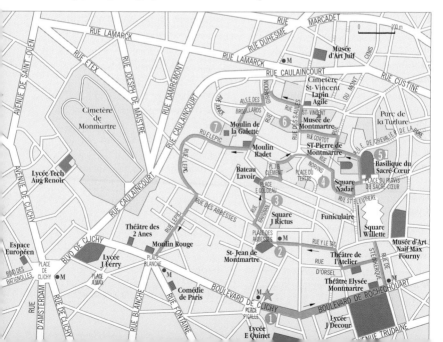

thought Saint-Denis was martyred in the 3rd century.

Notice the métro entrance on the place des Abbesses, with its glass-roofed, wrought-iron structure, originally designed by Hector Guimard at the turn of the 20th century. St-Jean l'Evangéliste, dating from the same period, was the first church to be built of concrete.

Leave by rue des Abbesses and turn right into the twisting rue Ravignan.

3 Place Emile-Goudeau

On this charming square is a reconstruction of the Bateau-Lavoir, burnt down in 1970, where Picasso and friends such as Braque, Modigliani, Juan Gris, and others made history (*see p78*).
Continue to the end of rue Ravignan. Follow rue Norvins.

4 Place du Tertre

Now focused on the tourist trade, this old village square has lost its authenticity, but you can just about imagine what it was like in the 1920s. The tiny place du Calvaire in the southwest corner offers exceptional views of the capital.
*Leave place du Tertre past the old church of St-Pierre (*see p75*) and walk to the Sacré-Coeur Basilica.*

5 Sacré-Coeur

If you don't mind crowds, you will enjoy the majesty of the place and the vast panorama in front (*see p100*).
*Walk across rue du Mont-Cenis and along rue Cortot where No. 12 houses the Musée de Montmartre (*see p75*). Turn right at the end of the street.*

6 Rue des Saules

This is one of the most picturesque streets, running downhill from the Butte. On the right is the Montmartre vineyard and, on the other side of rue St-Vincent, the Lapin Agile, hardly changed since the days of Picasso and Vlaminck. In the Cimetière St-Vincent opposite, you can see Utrillo's grave.
Walk along rue St-Vincent and turn left up some stairs to the Château des Brouillards, an 18th-century folly. Beyond is avenue Junot; turn left, then right into rue Lepic.

7 Moulin de la Galette

The old mill on your right was once a famous dance hall painted by Renoir and Van Gogh, who lived with his brother at No. 54.
Follow the street to the bottom of the hill. On the corner stands the Moulin Rouge.

Sacré-Coeur, atop Paris's highest point

Ever since the 12th century, when students and tutors rejected the stifling teaching of the church and moved to the Left Bank, Paris has been a centre of attraction for artists from all over the world, and the melting pot of new art movements. This long-standing tradition reached its climax during the second half of the 19th century.

It was after 1870 that Paris really became the world's artistic centre, being both a sanctuary for misunderstood artists, such as Oscar Wilde, and the birthplace of major art movements, such as Impressionism.

The 'Bateau-Lavoir' was the romantic name of a shabby wooden building in Montmartre, which at the turn of the century was lived in by poor artists including Modigliani, Van Dongen, Juan Gris, and, above all, Picasso and Braque, who developed the Cubist style as a reaction against Impressionism. Picasso's *Les Demoiselles d'Avignon* was painted

here. The artistic life is depicted in Puccini's opera *La Bohème*.

It was at that time too that Diaghilev created his *Ballets russes* and that the premiere of Stravinsky's *Sacre du Printemps* caused a scandal at the Théâtre des Champs Elysées. The indecisive period between 1918 and 1939 was marked by the 'lost generation', a group of American writers including Gertrude Stein, Ezra Pound, and Ernest Hemingway, while the Exposition Internationale des Arts Décoratifs et Industriels in 1925 launched a new style, Art Deco.

After the difficult post-World War II period, Paris is now reclaiming its position as leader in contemporary art. This revival was sparked off by the inauguration of the Centre Pompidou, followed by other major projects such as the Opéra Bastille and La Villette, which offer a new range of artistic experiences.

Paris remains, reassuringly, a city of street artists who can provide unique mementoes of your visit – perhaps you'll spot a budding Braque or Toulouse-Lautrec

Montparnasse

Unlike Montmartre, this 'other' artists' stronghold was brutally drawn into the 20th century when a major town-planning project remodelled its centre during the 1960s and 1970s.

Paris from the Tour Montparnasse

Olympian Heights

The area was jokingly given the pompous name of Mont Parnasse (Mount Parnassus) in the 17th century by students from the Latin Quarter. In the 18th century it was a place of popular entertainment as bars, restaurants, and cabarets, just outside the city boundaries, could serve tax-free wine. The tradition survived even after the district became part of Paris during the second half of the 19th century.

La 'Ruche'

Just before World War I, artists and poets suddenly moved from Montmartre to this unknown Left Bank district which soon came into the limelight, attracting painters and also composers such as Stravinsky and Satie, and later, the 'lost generation' of American writers. The wine pavilion from the 1900 Exposition Universelle was transferred to the passage de Dantzig by a patron of the arts for the benefit of needy artists; it was given the romantic name of la Ruche (the beehive), and soon welcomed Modigliani, Zadkine, Chagall, and Léger. Matisse, Picasso, Braque, Klee, Miró, Ernst, Cocteau, and Apollinaire all lived in Montparnasse at one time, their social life revolving round four cafés in

the boulevard Montparnasse: La Coupole, Le Select, La Rotonde, and Le Dôme. Here they met with Russian political refugees like Lenin and Trotsky.

The Old District

This is still centred round the Carrefour Vavin, now the place Pablo-Picasso, where the well-known café-restaurants have survived and keep the legend alive, crowded with today's intellectuals and artists. But, whereas the decor has been carefully preserved, the establishments are certainly more up-market now than in the days of Chagall. Just west of the Cimetière Montparnasse, rue de la Gaîté is, as its name implies, the centre of the district's nightlife. It is lined with cabarets, dance halls, and theatres such as the Théâtre de la Gaîté-Montparnasse and the Théâtre Montparnasse.

Cimetière de Montparnasse

The main entrance is in the boulevard Edgar-Quinet. Many writers, artists, and composers are buried here: among them the poet Baudelaire, the novelist Maupassant, the critic Sainte-Beuve, the philosopher Sartre and his lifelong companion Simone de Beauvoir, the composers César Franck and Saint-Saëns, and the sculptors Rude, Bourdelle, and Zadkine. On the eastern edge of the cemetery *The Kiss* is an interesting sculpture by the Romanian artist, Constantin Brancusi, who lived in Paris for many years.

Tour de Montparnasse
At the heart of the new development stands the 200-m high, 59-storey Tour de Maine-Montparnasse. When it was built in the early 1970s, it was Europe's tallest office block and raised fierce controversy. The fastest of the 25 lifts climbs 6m per second, reaching the top floor in 39 seconds. For most Parisians, the tower's only redeeming feature is the splendid panorama from the 56th and 59th floors. Across the pink-granite square in front of the tower is the new Gare Montparnasse.
33 avenue du Maine, 75015. Tel: 01 45 38 52 56. Open: 9.30am–11.30pm (10.30pm in winter). Admission charge.

Musée Bourdelle
The museum occupies the house and studio of Antoine Bourdelle, a disciple of Rodin, whose bust is among the exhibits. There are also some very interesting portraits of Beethoven.
16 rue Antoine-Bourdelle. Tel: 01 49 54 73 73. Open: 10am–5.40pm. Closed: Mon. Admission charge.

Musée de la Poste
The museum depicts the history of postal services, and has some fascinating exhibits such as the balloon used during the siege of Paris in 1870. There is also a collection of French stamps and a display of contemporary machines and methods.
34 boulevard de Vaugirard, 75015. Tel: 01 42 79 23 45; for group reservations tel: 01 42 79 24 24. Open: 10am–6pm. Closed: Sun. Admission charge. Métros: Montparnasse (exit place Bienvenue), Pasteúr, & Falguiére.

Musée Zadkine
The works of the Russian-born sculptor, Zadkine, are exhibited in the house where he lived for 40 years until his death in 1967. The majority of his works reveal his anxious nature. The various studies he made of Van Gogh are of particular interest.
100 bis rue d'Assas. Tel: 01 43 26 91 90. Open: 10am–5.30pm. Closed: Mon. Admission charge.

Rue de la Gaîté: old theatres survive despite the street's changing character

Musée d'Orsay

Ideally situated on the Left Bank, opposite the Jardins des Tuileries, the Musée d'Orsay has taken its rightful place among the top European art museums. It is an unusual museum, housed in a converted railway station, and this allowed the curators to depart from traditional display and to avoid monotony.

The elegant interior of the Musée d'Orsay

Gare d'Orsay

Inaugurated in 1900, the station was built on the site of the Palais d'Orsay which was burnt to the ground during the Commune of 1871. The architect, Victor Laloux, was entrusted with the delicate task of designing a station that would not deface the surrounding area, in particular the Louvre and Jardin des Tuileries just across the Seine. He concealed the glass-roofed iron structure behind a beautiful stone façade, and adorned it inside with an elaborately decorated, coffered ceiling. However, less than 40 years later it had become obsolete, its platforms being too short for new electric trains.

A Museum of 19th-Century Art

In 1977 it was decided to convert the station into an art museum that would re-group various collections covering the period from 1848 to 1914, including the famous Impressionist collection from the Jeu de Paume.

Thus, the new museum would make the link between the Louvre and the Musée National d'Art Moderne of the Pompidou Centre. It is an absolute must for anyone interested in 19th-century art.

The Museum

When the museum opened in 1986 after a number of setbacks, it was universally acclaimed for the originality of its excellent interior design.

The collections are exhibited in chronological order, on three main levels: the ground floor, the upper floor, and the middle floor (in that order). In addition to the permanent collections, there are temporary exhibitions. Ground plans and leaflets in English are available near the entrance.

The **ground floor** is devoted to the period from 1848 to 1880. The sculpture section, in the central gallery, illustrates an interesting progression from the classical style of Pradier *(Sapho)* to the Romantic approach of Carpeaux, who carved the beautiful figures of the Fontaine de l'Observatoire (*see p53*). The rooms on the right and left of the gallery form the painting section; on the right, the classical trend is represented by Ingres *(La Source)*, and the Romantic trend by Delacroix *(Chasse aux Lions)*. Further on, there are some fine Puvis de Chavannes and early Degas. The rooms on the left show the progression from realism, with Daumier, Millet *(Les Glaneuses)*, Courbet *(L'Atelier)*, and the

Barbizon school headed by Corot, towards Impressionism, represented by works painted before 1870: among them the famous *Déjeuner sur l'Herbe* by Manet, *La Pie* and *Femmes au Jardin* by Monet. In the architecture section, there is an interesting model of the Opéra Garnier and its district.

The **upper floor** is entirely devoted to Impressionism from 1872 and Post-Impressionism in a splendid festival of light and colour, with works by Monet, Renoir, Sisley, and Degas. Van Gogh, too, influenced by the movement, has his rightful place here; so does Cézanne, who stands apart as a pioneer of 20th-century painting.

Post-Impressionism is represented by Seurat, Toulouse-Lautrec, Henri Rousseau and his own naïve style, Gauguin and the school of Pont-Aven, Bonnard, Vuillard, and so on.

The **middle floor** painting section is devoted to Naturalism and Symbolism, which became officially recognised themes at a time when Impressionism was rejected, and to the early 20th century with artists such as Matisse and Bonnard.

The sculpture gallery presents works by Rodin and his successors. The Art Nouveau section is well headed by Gallé, Lalique, and Guimard.

1 rue de Bellechasse, 75007. Tel: 01 40 49 48 14. www.musee-orsay.Fr
Open: 10am–6pm (9am–6pm in summer), Thu 10am–9.45pm (less crowded early morning). Closed: Mon. Admission charge. Facilities include: ground floor – bookshop, post office, bureau de change, and cloakrooms; upper level – coffee shop; intermediate level – restaurant. Métro: Solférino.

A truly innovative restoration and renovation effort has given a new lease of life to the old Gare d'Orsay

Museums

The Paris Museum Pass enables you to visit over 70 museums and monuments in the Paris region. It is on sale at main métro stations, in participating museums, at monuments, and at the Musée et Compagnie (*see opposite page*).

Cité des Sciences et de l'Industrie
See p116.

Maison de Balzac
See pp114–15.

Musée de l'Armée
This is one of the most comprehensive military museums in the world. The collections are housed in buildings on either side of the main courtyard of Les Invalides (*see p57*).

The Musée de l'Armée

Galerie de l'Occident (west side)
Among the most remarkable exhibits in the ground-floor rooms is Henri II's suit of armour. The first floor is devoted to World War I and World War II, with a video film about D-Day.

Galerie de l'Orient (east side)
On the ground floor there are frescoes depicting Louis XIV's campaign in Flanders in 1672, and the famous paintings by Ingres of Napoleon on the day of his coronation. On the first floor there are mementoes of Napoleon. The second floor is devoted to the Second Empire and the Franco-Prussian war of 1870. A wing devoted to General de Gaulle and World War II opened in June 2000.
Hôtel des Invalides, 75007. Tel: 01 44 42 37 72. www. invalides.Fr

MODERN ART TRENDS

Fauvism: an early 20th-century trend characterised by a simplification of form and use of bright colours.

Cubism: an early 20th-century movement concerned with rendering form and volume through geometric shapes.

Abstract Art: a movement started in 1910 by Kandinsky and rejecting figurative representation of reality. Developed mainly from 1950 onwards, especially in the US with Abstract Expressionism.

Surrealism: a 1920s trend that rejected all conventions and aimed at expressing the subconscious mind.

Realism and New Realism: from 1960 onwards, they mark a return to figurative painting with the introduction of objects from everyday life.

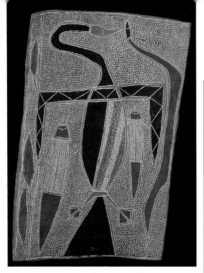

Display in the Musée des Arts d'Afrique et d'Océanie

Open: 10am–5pm (6pm in summer). Admission charge. Métro: Invalides.

Musée d'Art Moderne de la Ville de Paris

The museum is housed in the Palais de Tokyo. *La Fée Electricité*, painted by Dufy for the occasion, is exhibited in the museum, alongside other works of 20th- and 21st-century art. *(Also see p95.)*
Palais de Tokyo, 11 avenue du Président-Wilson, 75016. Tel: 01 53 67 40 00. www.paris-France.org/MUSEES Open: 10am–5.45pm (6.45pm at weekends). Closed: Mon. Admission charge. Métro: Alma-Marceau.

Musée des Arts d'Afrique et d'Océanie

See p123.

Musée des Arts Asiatiques-Guimet

Founded in the 19th century by Emile Guimet, the museum now houses a major collection of Far Eastern art on three floors. Exhibits are from India,

Cambodia, Pakistan, Afghanistan, and China. On the second floor there are some beautiful Chinese ceramics.
19 avenue d'Iéna, 75016. Tel: 01 56 52 53 00. www.museeguimet.Fr Open: 9.45am–6pm. Closed: Tue. Admission charge. Métro: Iéna.

Musée des Arts Décoratifs

The collections are chronologically presented in the north wing of the Louvre. The 20th-century section includes a splendid reconstruction of Jeanne Lanvin's flat, some Dubuffet paintings and sculptures, and glass objects by Gallé and Lalique. There is also a large toy collection.
107 rue de Rivoli, 75001. Tel: 01 44 55 57 50. Open: 11am–6pm (9pm Wed). Closed: Mon. Admission charge. Métro: Palais-Royal or Tuileries. (The museum is partially closed for renovation and a full reopening is scheduled for 2003.)

Musée de la Mode et du Textile

Housed in the Pavillon de Marsan, the museum depicts the history of fashion and costume from the Middle Ages to the present day.
107 rue de Rivoli, 75001. Tel: 01 44 55 57 50. www.ucad.Fr Open: 11am–6pm (9pm Wed). Closed: Mon. Admission charge. Métro: Palais-Royal or Tuileries.

Musée des Arts et Traditions Populaires (*see p113*).
Musée Bourdelle (*see p81*).
Musée Cernuschi (*see p113*).
Musée de la Chasse et de la Nature (*see p71*).
Musée et Compagnie 49 rue Etienne Marcel, 75001. Open: 10am–6.30pm. Closed: Sun. Métro: Etienne-Marcel.

Musée National du Moyen Age – Thermes de Cluny

Housed in one of the few domestic medieval buildings left in Paris, on the site of ancient Roman baths *(see p61)*, this is an exceptionally fine museum entirely devoted to the Middle Ages.

On the ground floor there are 15th- and 16th-century tapestries made in Holland in the *mille fleurs* style. Particularly worthy of note is a set called *La Vie Seigneuriale*, depicting the life of the aristocracy in the 16th century.

In room VIII, there are some fragments of sculpture, including 21 heads from the Galerie des Rois that were originally on the west front of Notre-Dame. Next door is the well-preserved *frigidarium* with a fine example of Roman vaulting.

On the first floor is the museum's major exhibit: a set of six tapestries from the late-15th century, called *La Dame à la Licorne* (the Lady and the Unicorn). The lovely Gothic chapel contains another set of tapestries illustrating the life of St Stephen.
6 place Paul-Painlevé, 75005.
Tel: 01 53 73 78 16.
www.musee-moyenage.Fr
Open: 9.15am–5.45pm. Closed: Tue.
Admission charge.
Métro: Cluny-La Sorbonne, St-Michel, or Odéon.

Musée Cognacq-Jay

This collection of 18th-century art has found a proper setting in the recently renovated Hôtel Donon in the Marais. Paintings and pastels by Boucher, Fragonard, La Tour, Greuze, Tiepolo, and Reynolds, and drawings by Watteau are enhanced by fine pieces of furniture and other objects of the same period.
8 rue Elzévir, 75003. Tel: 01 40 27 07 21.
Open: 10am–5.40pm. Closed: Mon.
Admission charge. Métro: St-Paul.

Musée Delacroix,
See p107.

Musée Grévin

This waxworks, founded in 1882, provides good entertainment for the whole family. There are vivid historical scenes, and numerous life-size wax figures of famous people, as well as distorting mirrors.
10 boulevard Montmartre, 75009.
Tel: 01 47 70 85 05. www.musee-grevin.Fr
Open: 10am–7pm. Admission charge.
Métro: rue Montmartre.

Musée Gustave Moreau
See p114.

Musée de l'Histoire de Paris

Housed in the imposing Hôtel Carnavalet, the museum was recently extended to the Hôtel Le-Peletier-de-St-Fargeau, and covers the history of Paris from its origins to the present day.

Hôtel Carnavalet

The museum is reached through the monumental doorway and across the courtyard with an equestrian statue of Louis XIV by Coysevox. There are some interesting scenes from Paris life in the 16th century, supported by a host of details such as shop and inn signs. Upstairs are reconstructed rooms from the reigns of Louis XIV, XV, and XVI, and Madame de Sévigné's apartments.

Hôtel Le-Peletier-de-St-Fargeau

This is linked to the Hôtel Carnavalet, and covers the period from the French Revolution; start on the second floor. There are models of the Bastille and the guillotine, and everyday life objects, as well as a reconstruction of the Temple prison where Louis XVI was held. The ground floor deals with the first half of the 19th century through portraits of people in the limelight. The first floor follows on with the Second Empire and the great architectural schemes that were carried out during that period. The lifestyle of the early 20th century is presented through reconstructions of rooms such as Marcel Proust's bedroom. *23 rue de Sévigné, 75003. Tel: 01 44 59 58 58. Open: 10am–5.40pm. Closed: Mon. Admission charge. Métro: St-Paul.*

Musée de L'Histoire de France

This museum, housed in the beautiful Hôtel de Soubise, depicts French history through documents selected from the national archives. Of particular interest are the Edit de Nantes of 1598 recognising religious freedom, and its Révocation in 1685, which led to the exile of the Huguenots; the Déclaration des Droits de l'Homme of 1789 (Declaration of Human Rights); Louis XVI's diary; Napoleon's will, and many others. The apartments of the Princess de Soubise have the most exquisite Rococo decorations, with paintings by Natoire, Boucher, and Van Loo. *60 rue des Francs Bourgeois, 75003. Tel: 01 44 59 58 58. Open: 10am–5.45pm (1.45–5.45pm on weekends). Closed: Tue. Admission charge. Métro: Rambuteau.*

Façade of old café, Musée Carnavalet

Musée de l'Homme

This museum of mankind, housed in the vast Palais de Chaillot, depicts the evolution of the human race since the origin of the species, and presents a comparative study of the different races in their traditional cnvironment.

17 place du Trocadéro, 75016. Tel: 01 44 05 72 72. Open: 9.45am–5.15pm. Closed: Tue. Admission charge. Métro: Trocadéro.

Institut du Monde Arabe

The building situated along the river, facing the Ile St-Louis, is the result of close cooperation between France and 19 Arab countries with the aim of promoting cultural exchanges between Islam and the West. The institute houses a reference centre, a video centre, a comprehensive library, research facilities, and a museum (on the 7th floor) which illustrates Arab civilisation from the 9th century onwards. The south façade consists of 1,600 identical metal light screens which electronically filter the sunlight as it enters the building. From the cafeteria on the 9th floor there are lovely views of the river.

Rue des Fossés St-Bernard, 75005. Tel: 01 40 51 38 38. www.imarabe.org Open: 10am–6pm. Closed: Mon. Admission charge. Métro: Jussieu or Cardinal-Lemoine.

Musée Jacquemart André

Situated right in the centre of town, but a little off the visitor's beaten track, this elegant 1870 mansion houses fine collections of Renaissance and 18th-century art, displayed in beautiful surroundings. They include portraits by Gainsborough and Reynolds, paintings and drawings by Rubens, Rembrandt, Van Dyck, Frans Hals, and Ruysdaël, 16th-century enamels and ceramics, some beautiful furniture, Beauvais tapestries, and paintings by Boucher and Watteau.

158 boulevard Haussmann, 75008. Tel: 01 45 62 11 59. Closed: Mon. Admission charge. Métro: St-Philippe-du-Roule or Miromesnil.

Musée de la Marine

Founded in 1827 by Charles X, the museum now occupies the west wing of the Palais de Chaillot. With the help of scale models and actual crafts, it illustrates all kinds of maritime transport from battleships to pleasure

Poster announcing an exhibition

boats. There is an interesting royal toy called *Louis XV*, Marie Antoinette's pleasure boat at Versailles, a rowing boat specially built for Napoleon in 1811, and the *Belle Poule* in which his remains were brought back to France from the island of St Helena. The *Gloire*, dating from 1859, was the first armoured warship in the world. And, of course, exhibits include ships used for exploration, such as the *Astrolabe*, which took Dumont d'Urville to the Antarctic in the 19th century, and mementoes of the great explorers La Pérouse, Brazza, and Charcot. Temporary exhibitions are a regular feature.

Place du Trocadéro, 75016. Tel: 01 53 65 69 69. Open: 10am–5.50pm. Closed: Tue. Admission charge. Métro: Trocadéro.

Musée Marmottan

This is a strange museum which, as a result of various bequests, has developed from the original private collection into an original museum of Impressionist painting. It bears the name of the art historian Paul Marmottan, who, in 1932, donated his house and private collections to the Académie des Beaux-Arts. These included Renaissance tapestries, furniture, and sculpture, as well as early 19th-century paintings and objets d'art.

Following other legacies, the museum acquired some beautiful medieval manuscripts, and its first Impressionist paintings, including Monet's famous *Impression: Sunrise* (1872), which gave the movement its name.

However, the outstanding asset of the museum is the collection of 65 paintings by Monet donated by his son in 1971.

Floating work of art, Musée de la Marine

Exhibited in a specially built under-ground gallery, they testify to Monet's love of his country home in Giverny (*see p127*). The different moods of his garden are rendered with supreme mastery. The studies of water lilies, for instance, show the master's obsessive progression towards the huge canvases exhibited in the Orangerie museum (*see p90*).

2 rue Louis-Boilly, 75016. Tel: 01 44 96 50 33. www.marmottan.com Open: 10am–5.30pm. Closed: Mon. Admission charge. Métro: La Muette.

Musée du Louvre (*see pp66–7*).
Musée des Lunettes et des Lorgnettes (*see p114*).

Musée de la Musique
See p117.

Musée de l'Orangerie
The south pavilion on the place de la Concorde houses a substantial collection of paintings from the Impressionist period to the early 20th century, but it is mostly renowned for Monet's *Nymphéas*.

There are some remarkable still lifes by Cézanne, some delightful portraits by Renoir, and paintings by Picasso, Derain, Modigliani, and Matisse, as well as a few of Henri Rousseau's best naïve works, including *La Carriole du Père Junier.*

Monet's huge *Nymphéas* (Water Lilies), painted at Giverny, are exhibited on the ground floor in two oval rooms, according to the instructions given by the artist himself.
Place de la Concorde, 75001. Tel: 01 42 97 48 16. Currenty being refurbished, scheduled to reopen in 2003. Métro: Concorde.

Musée Picasso
The ornate elegance of the 17th-century Hôtel Salé makes a perfect background for the works of a great master of 20th-century art. The building was renovated recently to accommodate a collection of Picasso's works donated to the state by his heirs in lieu of death duties: 200 paintings, more than 150 sculptures, 3,000 drawings and engravings, and 88 ceramics.

Picasso's personal collection of works by other major artists of his time, such as Cézanne, Derain, Braque, Miró, Rousseau, and Matisse, was also donated to the state by Jacqueline Picasso.

Picasso's prodigious output is presented in chronological order, starting on the first floor with the 'blue period' (*Autoportrait*), followed by the Cubist period (*Nature morte à la chaise cannée*).

Musée Rodin: works shown outdoors

Mecca for art lovers – the Musée Picasso

The period between World War I and World War II is illustrated by such paintings as *Paul en arlequin, Le Baiser, Femme lisant,* and the famous *Portrait de Dora Maar.* Among Picasso's post-war production, the series of studies on Manet's *Déjeuner sur l'Herbe* is particularly remarkable.

Some of Picasso's sculptures are exhibited in the garden, where there is also a pleasant café.
5 rue de Thorigny, 75003. Tel: 01 42 71 25 21. Open: 9.30am–6pm. Closed: Tue. Admission charge. Métro: St-Paul.

Musée Rodin

The superb collection of Rodin's sculptures is exhibited in the Hôtel Biron, where he lived from 1907 until his death in 1917. Some of his works, in bronze and white marble, are in the house, while others are distributed round the beautiful garden. A visit on a sunny day is highly recommended. In the garden are two of his most famous works: *Le Penseur* and *Les Bourgeois de Calais,* as well as *La Porte de l'Enfer* and *Ugolin.* On the ground floor there are more masterpieces, such as *Le Baiser* and *La Cathédrale.* On the first floor are the plaster casts used for the statues of Balzac and Victor Hugo.
77 rue de Varenne, 75007.
Tel: 01 44 18 16 10. www.musee-rodin.Fr
Open: 9.30am–5.45pm. Closed: Mon. Admission charge. Métro: Varenne.

Musée de la Monnaie (*see p106*).
Musée de Montmartre (*see p75*).
Musée National d'Art Moderne
(*see pp36–7*).
Musée Nissim de Camondo (*see p114*).
Musée d'Orsay (*see pp82–3*).
Musée du Petit Palais (*see p26*).
Musée de la Poste (*see p81*).
Musée Seita (*see p114*).
Musée de la Serrure (*see p73*).
Musée Victor Hugo (*see p99*).
Musée du Vin (*see p115*).
Musée Zadkine (*see p81*).
Palais de la Découverte (*see p26*).
Pavillon de l'Arsenal (*see p29*).

Notre-Dame

The harmonious strength of the cathedral's outline, the proportions of its façade, the subtle combination of simplicity and refinement in its design, are undoubtedly the perfect expression of French Gothic architecture. Notre-Dame is the nucleus round which the capital developed, and major celebrations, often marking a turning point in French history, were staged in the cathedral.

Detail of roof. The view from the top is truly spectacular

Bishop Maurice de Sully

In 1163, Bishop de Sully launched the building process that lasted nearly 200 years. The architects, Jean de Chelles and Pierre de Montreuil, worked on it during the 13th century, when the Ste-Chapelle was also built. The building was completed in 1345 with the flying buttresses surrounding the chancel.

Notre-Dame Today

Although the cathedral never suffered spectacular damage, by the mid-19th century it had been deprived of some of its magnificent sculptures, and the edifice was in serious need of repair. Restoration work was carried out under the care of Viollet-le-Duc, and the cathedral regained its past splendour. Haussmann later widened the Parvis (square) in front of it to increase the dramatic effect of its unique setting.

Today, two other vantage points, the square Jean XXIII behind the chancel, and the square Viviani on the Left Bank, reveal the perfect proportions of the edifice, which is 130m long and 49m wide. Its towers rise to a height of 68m.

The Façade

The façade is the most striking part of the building. The heavily restored central portal depicts the *Last Judgement*, and the upper part shows Christ surrounded by the celestial court. The portal of the Virgin on the left has a particularly beautiful tympanum illustrating the coronation of the Virgin Mary. The sculptures on the portal of St Anne on the right are the oldest in the cathedral; the remarkable tympanum again shows the Virgin Mary with Bishop Maurice de Sully, founder of the cathedral, at her side. The lintel depicts scenes from the life of St Anne.

The rose window is over 700 years old. Birds and demons were placed at the base of the towers by Viollet-le-Duc in true Gothic spirit.

The great bell in the south tower, weighing 13 tonnes, is heard only on special occasions. The view from the top is rewarding if you have the courage to climb the 386 steps. The portal on the south side has a 13th-century tympanum, which depicts the martyr St Stephen. The slightly earlier north portal by Jean de Chelles was adorned with a statue of the Virgin and Child, but the child is now missing.

The Interior

The vast interior can accommodate up to 9,000 people. The 35-m high nave is separated from the chancel by a wide transept, which has two magnificent rose windows.

The chancel was redecorated in the 17th century as the result of a vow made by Louis XIII if he were granted an heir. A *pietà* by Coysevox stands in the centre, with statues of Louis XIII and Louis XIV on either side. On the right of the chancel, the treasury houses some old relics, including a fragment of the Cross.

Place du Parvis Notre-Dame, 75004. Tel: 01 42 34 56 10. Open: 8am–6.45pm (7.45pm weekends). Métro: St-Michel or Cité. RER: St-Michel-Notre-Dame. Treasury open: 2.30am–6pm; closed: Sun. Admission charge. Towers open: winter 10am–5.30pm, spring & autumn 9am–8pm, till 9pm in summer. Admission charge.

Nearby

Ste-Chapelle, Conciergerie, Churches of St-Julien-le-Pauvre and St-Séverin, Musée Nationale du Moyen Age–Thermes de Cluny, Ile St-Louis.

The cathedral as it appears from the River Seine

The Jardin du Palais-Royal

Opera Garnier

The architecture of this ornately decorated opera house epitomises the elaborate style of the 1860s. It was designed by Charles Garnier, a young and still unknown architect, who won the competition because of the boldness of his plans, which departed from the usual Neo-Classical style. When the Opéra was inaugurated in 1875, its vast stage, able to accommodate nearly 500 artists, ranked it among the world's finest opera houses.

Groups of statues by various artists welcome the spectators at the top of the steps at the main entrance. One of them, *la Danse* by Carpeaux, considered highly immoral at the time, has been replaced by a copy. The original is in the Musée d'Orsay.

The auditorium, which seats around 2,000, has red and gold as the dominant colours. The ceiling was painted by Chagall during the 1960s. The huge chandelier hanging in the centre weighs nearly 7 tonnes.

Place de l'Opéra, 75002. Tel: 01 40 01 22 63. Open: daily, summer 10am–6pm, winter 10am–5pm. Closed: during special events. Métro: Opéra.

Palais de Chaillot

This site has been much sought after for its superb views of the river and the Left Bank. Catherine de Médicis had a country house built on the colline de Chaillot (Chaillot hill).

In 1937, the present building was erected for the Exposition Universelle. Twin pavilions with curved wings are separated by a vast terrace beneath which is the Théâtre National de Chaillot, one of the leading French theatres (entrance through the east pavilion). The palace houses three museums, Musée de l'Homme, Musée de la Marine (*see pp88–9*), and Musée des Monuments Français (currently closed).
*Place du Trocadéro, 75016.
Métro: Trocadéro.*

Palais-Royal

The palace was commissioned in 1624 by Richelieu, who was then Louis XIII's minister. It became a *palais royal* (royal palace) when he left it to the king in his will. Louis XIV then gave it to his brother, Philippe d'Orléans, whose descendants surrounded the garden with shopping arcades and apartments and built the Comédie-Française. Cafés, restaurants, gambling houses, and dance halls thrived within its precinct until, in the mid-19th century, Louis-Philippe took the fun out of the area by closing the gambling houses. The palace is not open to the public, but you can go through the main courtyard, invaded by

the black and white Colonnes de Buren (pillars), into the peaceful garden surrounded by dainty boutiques.
Place du Palais-Royal.
Métro: Palais-Royal.

Palais de Tokyo

Situated a short distance upriver from the Palais de Chaillot, the Palais de Tokyo was also built for the 1937 Exposition Universelle in much the same style. The palace houses the Musée d'Art Moderne de la Ville de Paris and a new arts centre (*see p85*), and the surrounding terraces are decorated with statues by Emile Bourdelle.
11 avenue du Président-Wilson, 75016.
Métro: Alma-Marceau.

The Comédie Française
This famous theatre company was founded by Louis XIV in 1680, a few years after Molière's death, with the aim of combining two rival theatre companies. Frowned upon by the Sorbonne, it was forced to move several times, until Napoleon made it an official institution with a director appointed by the State. Its repertoire is traditionally classical, but also includes works by modern authors, both French and foreign. In the foyer is the chair that Molière collapsed into during a performance of *Le Malade Imaginaire*.

A series of pools fronts the Palais de Chaillot, across the river from the Eiffel Tower

Walk: From the Opéra to the Palais-Royal

The prestigious Opéra House and the elegant Palais-Royal epitomise the impression of refinement and grandeur that one gets from this walk.

Allow 2 hours.

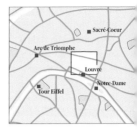

Begin from the place de l'Opéra (métro Opéra). Cross the boulevard des Capucines, then turn right.

1 Rue de la Paix

Named rue Napoléon when it was opened in 1806, it is today lined with expensive jewellers (the famous Cartier is at No. 13) and has become the symbol of luxury. It leads into the elegant place Vendôme, which Napoleon admires from the top of the central column.

Cross the square, walk along rue de Castiglione and turn left.

2 Rue St-Honoré

The Carré des Feuillants on the corner of the rue de Castiglione is a fashionable but expensive restaurant where you can experiment with *la nouvelle çuisine*. The church of St-Roch halfway down the street stood on a hillock known as the Butte Saint-Roch, which was completely levelled for the building of the avenue de l'Opéra: before that, you had to go down seven steps to gain access to the church; now you have to go up 13!

Further along the street on the right, rue des Pyramides leads to the square which bears the same name, with a gilded statue of Joan of Arc, erected in the 19th century on the very spot where she was wounded while attempting to deliver Paris from English occupation. *Follow rue St-Honoré which leads to the Palais-Royal.*

3 Palais-Royal

As you reach the place André-Malraux, you get a splendid view of the Opéra to your left. Across the square is the Théâtre-Français, home of the famous Comédie-Française *(see p94)*. Close by is place Colette, from where you enter the Palais-Royal gardens. Before you do, however, carry on a little further to the Louvre des Antiquaires, which has 250 shops and a convenient restaurant. *Walk through the Jardin du Palais-Royal. Turn right into rue des Petits-Champs and, if you are ready for a meal, try the Mercure Galant at No. 15.*

4 Galeries Colbert and Vivienne

These charming covered arcades date from the early 19th century; the Galerie Vivienne is the most beautiful of the two, with its carved, vaulted ceiling and glass roof, and old-fashioned bookshop. *Rue des Petits-Champs leads to the circular place des Victoires with a statue of Louis XIV in the centre* (see p109). *Leave by rue Vide-Gousset.*

5 Notre-Dame-des-Victoires

The 17th-century church is famous for its paintings, its monument to Lully, and more than 30,000 ex-votos on the walls. *Continue along rue Notre-Dame-des-Victoires, turn left past the Palais de la Bourse (the Stock Exchange), then left again into rue de Richelieu.*

6 Bibliothèque Nationale

Under French law, publishers are required to submit several copies of all works they publish at the Bibliothèque. Since 1992, computerised and multi-media documents are also required to be submitted. To help house this exhaustive collection, a new facility has been built at the François Mitterand site in the 13th *arrondissement.*

7 Fontaine Molière

Further along rue de Richelieu, you will see a 19th-century fountain, dedicated to Molière, not far from the house (now No. 40) where he died in 1673 after collapsing on stage. *Turn right into rue Thérèse, then follow rue Ste-Anne back to rue des Petits-Champs; on the corner stands Lully's house adorned with musical motives. Walk back along avenue de l'Opéra.*

Nearby
Musée Grévin, La Madeleine, Palais du Louvre, Jardin des Tuileries.

Panthéon

This vast monument towering over the Latin Quarter tends to dwarf everything around it, particularly the beautiful church of St-Etienne-du-Mont. Looked at from a distance, however, the harmonious proportions of its high dome, underlined by an elegant ring of slender columns, make it a splendid example of Neo-Classical architecture.

St Geneviève Church

When, in 1744, Louis XV suffered a serious illness, he vowed to build a beautiful new church to replace the ancient church of St Geneviève Abbey. After his recovery, he commissioned the architect, Soufflot, who designed a magnificent building in the shape of a Greek cross, with a huge dome 83m high; the saint's shrine would be placed beneath it.

The Panthéon, where the illustrious rest

Work began in 1758, but was only completed after Soufflot's death in 1789, on the eve of the Revolution.

The Panthéon

In 1791, the Assemblée Constituante decided that all the nation's 'great men' should be buried inside the church, which was renamed Panthéon after the Greek and Roman temples dedicated to all the gods. However, with the return of the monarchy, the building became a church once again until, in 1885, the decision was finally taken to restore it to its role of national mausoleum, in honour of the writer Victor Hugo who had just died.

The Interior

Forty-two of the original windows were blocked up in 1791 and the bare walls were later decorated with scenes depicting the life of St Geneviève by Puvis de Chavannes, and paintings by other late-19th-century artists.

In the vast crypt are the tombs of some of France's 'great men': Voltaire, Rousseau, Hugo, Zola, the Resistance leader Jean Moulin, Jean Monnet, usually referred to as the 'father of Europe', and many others.

Place du Panthéon, 75005. Tel: 01 44 32 18 00. Open: 9.30am– 6.30pm, winter 10am–6.15pm. Admission charge. Métro: Cardinal-Lemoine. RER: Luxembourg.

Place des Vosges

This beautiful square is a refreshing haven compared with the magnificent place de la Concorde or the supremely elegant place Vendôme. Its sober yet

Victor Hugo's house, place des Vosges

extremely refined architecture gives it a kind of exquisite charm.

Commissioned by Henri IV at the beginning of the 17th century, the square was inaugurated after his death by his son Louis XIII and named place Royale. The two higher buildings, in the centre of the south and north sides, are called Pavillon du Roi (King's Pavilion) and Pavillon de la Reine (Queen's Pavilion) respectively, though they were never inhabited by the royal family. In the central garden stands a statue of Louis XIII. The square was renamed place des Vosges in 1800.

Some of the other residences have been lived in by famous people: Madame de Sévigné was born at No. 1 bis in 1626, Cardinal Richelieu occupied No. 21 before he moved to the Palais-Royal, and Victor Hugo lived in No. 6 from 1832 to 1848, before his exile to Jersey and Guernsey. The house is now a museum with various mementoes of his life: furniture, objects he collected, portraits and photographs, and also drawings by Hugo himself.

Musée Victor Hugo, 6 place des Vosges, 75004. Tel: 01 42 72 10 16. Open: Tue–Sun 10am–5.40pm. Closed: Mon. Admission charge. Métro: St-Paul.

Place Vendôme

Built at the end of the 17th century by Jules Hardouin-Mansart, this imposing square is a magnificent example of the Louis XIV style.

Here again, symmetry is the overriding principle: a terrace of mansions over a row of arcades, with an original feature designed to break the monotony. The central buildings and those cutting the four corners are surmounted by pediments. Chopin died at No. 12, and No. 15 is now the prestigious Ritz Hotel; famous jewellers are established all round the square.

The central column that replaced the equestrian statue of Louis XIV was erected by Napoleon to celebrate his victory at Austerlitz.

The statue at the top was changed many times until the Third Republic finally settled on a copy of the original, representing Napoleon dressed as a Roman *(see p96)*.

Métro: Tuileries or Opéra.

Les Quais

The *quais* (embankments) are the city's main thoroughfares, carrying fast-moving traffic from east to west and vice versa. Lined with wide pavements planted with trees, the *quais* offer lovely walks along the river with fine views of the monuments situated on both banks of the Seine and on the Ile-de-la-Cité:

The Right Bank

The quai de la Mégisserie and the quai de Gesvres are lined with picturesque pet shops. From here there is a splendid view across the river of the Conciergerie on the Ile-de-la-Cité. The tiny square de l'Ave Maria offers an interesting view of the medieval Hôtel de Sens. Across the Pont Marie is the Ile St-Louis.

The Left Bank

There are striking views of Notre-Dame from the quai de la Tournelle, and from the quai de Montebello; just off the latter is the delightful square René-Viviani. Past the place St-Michel, the quai des Grands-Augustins, named after a nearby monastery, is lined with second-hand bookstalls on the riverside, and has a couple of 17th-century mansions on the other side. The Pont-Neuf, the oldest bridge in Paris, is in two sections, and joins the Right and Left Banks to the Ile-de-la-Cité.
Métro: Pont-Neuf, Châtelet, Pont Marie & St-Michel.

Sacré-Coeur

Visible from almost anywhere in Paris, the white basilica has become one of the city's most famous landmarks *(see p77)*. The decision to build it was taken by the Assemblée Nationale in 1873, to boost public morale after the Franco-Prussian War. Work started in 1875, but the building was only completed in 1914, and consecrated after World War I. The architecture is a bit disappointing, but its Byzantine style makes it instantly recognisable on the skyline. The mosaic decorating the chancel vaulting is impressive. It is possible to go up to the top of the dome for a superb view of Paris.
Parvis du Sacré-Coeur, 75018. Tel: 01 53 41 89 00. Dome open: 9am–6pm. Admission charge. Métro: Anvers, then access by funicular.

Ste-Chapelle

The distinctive, 75-m high spire in the sky reveals from a distance the presence of this jewel of Gothic architecture, partly hidden by the Palais de Justice buildings. In 1239, Louis IX, better known as St-Louis, acquired the Crown of Thorns from the Emperor of Constantinople, together with other precious relics,

LES BOUQUINISTES

Second-hand bookstalls are one of the familiar sights of Paris, and a stroll along the river would be less enjoyable without them. The tattered, green-painted boxes that used to be carried to and fro by their owners have become permanent fixtures. At night they are locked, but in the afternoon they open one by one, like stranded sea shells, revealing books, prints, postcards, and maps. A browse under their precariously propped-up lids is always fun, although there are not many rare editions or bargains to be found anymore!

including a fragment of the True Cross, and immediately decided to build a special shrine to house them in the courtyard of the royal palace. Pierre de Montreuil was entrusted with this delicate task. The Ste-Chapelle was built in less than three years and consecrated in 1248. After the Revolution, it was no longer used as a church, and the relics were transferred to Notre-Dame where they are now kept in the Treasury.

In order to let in as much light as possible, the vaulted roof was supported by thin pillars which were separated by long, narrow stained-glass windows 15m high. A few buttresses help reinforce the structure, which appears to have no walls. The narrow edifice consists of two

chapels, one above the other. The *chapelle basse* (lower chapel), is richly decorated, and its floor paved with tombstones. A spiral staircase leads to the *chapelle haute* (upper chapel), which appears wrapped in a blaze of light and colour. The huge stained-glass windows are undoubtedly the most striking feature: still mainly 13th-century, they are the oldest in Paris, depicting over 1,000 scenes from the Old and New Testaments in great detail.

4 boulevard du Palais, 75004. Tel: 01 53 73 78 50. Open: daily, summer 9.30am–6pm, winter 10am–5pm. Admission charge. Access through the Cour de Mai of the Palais de Justice. Métro: St-Michel or Cité.

The Sacré-Coeur, today a city landmark

Walk: Rive Droite, Rive Gauche

This takes you from the 'royal' Tuileries Gardens across the river to the Faubourg St Germain, once fashionable with the aristocracy, whose splendid mansions have now been taken over by ministries and embassies.

Allow 2 hours (excluding visit to Musée d'Orsay).

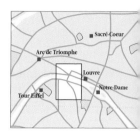

1 Rue de Rivoli

The elegant arcades, once lined with smart shops, now house souvenir shops. The hotel Meurice, at No. 228, served as headquarters of the German high command during World War II.

Enter the Tuileries Gardens on your right.

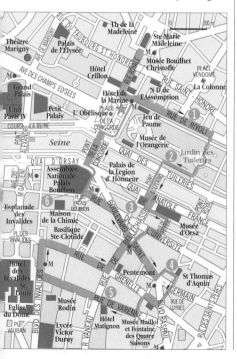

2 Jardin des Tuileries

Laid out in 1664 by Louis XIV's chief gardener, André Le Nôtre, the gardens soon became a popular place for strolling. The western end is quite elaborate, with its octagonal pool surrounded by statues, terraces, and twin pavilions, while from the round pool at the other end, the view extends all the way to the Champs Elysées and the Arc de Triomphe.

The Terrasse du Bord de l'Eau, by the river, affords good views of the Left Bank. Cross the Pont de Solferino.

3 Palais de la Légion d'Honneur

Take rue Bellechasse between the impressive Musée d'Orsay (left), which has a convenient restaurant, and the Musée de la Légion d'Honneur (right) which illustrates the history of the orders of French Chivalry before the 1789 Revolution, and the Legion of Honour which was founded by Napoleon in 1802.

Tel: 01 40 62 84 25. Open: Tue–Sun 2–5pm. Closed: Mon.

Turn left into rue de Lille. Rue de Poitiers leads to the rue de l'Université. On reaching the boulevard St-Germain, turn left, then turn left again into rue du Bac.

4 St-Thomas-d'Aquin

Begun in the 17th century and finished in the 18th, this church, on the right, was originally the chapel of a Dominican monastery. Inside are some fine 17th- and 18th-century paintings, which provide a perfect setting for the regular Sunday organ concerts.

Follow rue de Luynes to rue de Grenelle, and turn right past the elaborate Fontaine des Quatre Saisons (see p53). Turn left.

5 Rue de Varenne

The name of the street is derived from *gerenne* (warren), a reminder of the days when Faubourg was a rural area. It is lined with several stately mansions: the most famous is the Hôtel Matignon at No. 57, the prime minister's official residence since 1958. Built in 1721 and once owned by Talleyrand, it has the largest private gardens in Paris. Its contemporary, the Hôtel Biron at the end of the street, also has beautiful gardens. Today the building houses a museum dedicated to the sculptor Rodin, who lived there.

Turn right, then right again into rue de Grenelle, taking a look at the smaller-scale Hôtel de Lillars at No. 118.

6 Palais Bourbon

The rue de Bellechasse and the boulevard St-Germain bring you back to the river, past the impressive Palais Bourbon (seat of the Assemblée Nationale), remodelled by Napolean to match the Madeleine facing it on the other side of the place de la Concorde.

Cross the Pont de la Concorde and the place de la Concorde, then follow rue Royale towards the Madeleine.

Nearby
Rue du Faubourg-St-Honoré, Place Vendôme, Invalides, Pont Alexandre.

Former platforms of the Musée d'Orsay – now a gallery showing the art of the Impressionists

The jewel-like beauty of Ste-Chapelle

St-Germain-des-Prés

Situated on the Left Bank, next to the Latin Quarter, St-Germain-des-Prés has, since the days of Sartre and the Existentialists, been known as the rallying place of the intellectual avant-garde, who traditionally met in the literary cafés of the boulevard St-Germain.

The district nestles round the ancient church of St-Germain des Prés *(see p41)* and abounds in interesting contrasts. The wide boulevard St-Germain, cutting right across it and carrying fast traffic eastwards, spoils the immediate surroundings of the church a bit, but the backstreets are delightful, each having its own attractive feature. There is the rue de Buci with its lively open-air market, and the very old streets in the vicinity of the quaint place de Fürstemberg, rue Cardinale, rue de l'Echaudé, going back to the 14th century, and rue Bourbon-le-Château.

Further west, rue Bonaparte and rue des Sts-Pères, running down to the river, are lined with old-fashioned antique shops and art galleries, while rue Jacob, at right angles to them, is one of the most pleasant streets in the area. On the busy boulevard St-Germain, near the place St-Germain-des-Prés, are the well-known cafés closely associated with the district, the Café des Deux Magots and the Café de Flore.
Métro: St-Germain-des-Prés or Mabillon.

Ste-Marie Madeleine

This church in the guise of a Greek temple is known

(see p41)

LITERARY CAFÉS

Several cafés near the church of St-Germain des Prés have been the rendezvous of intellectuals and artists. The Procope, rue de l'Ancienne-Comédie, just off the Carrefour de l'Odéon, is the oldest. It was opened in 1686, by a Sicilian whose excellent coffee drew actors from the Comédie-Française opposite. Later, it attracted philosophers such as Voltaire and Rousseau, revolutionaries like Danton, Robespierre, and Marat, and famous 19th-century writers and poets, Musset, George Sand, Balzac, and Hugo. The claim to fame of the Flore and the Deux Magots is much more recent. In the late 1940s and 1950s, they became the haunt of Sartre, Simone de Beauvoir, Camus, Prévert, and the post-war generation of philosophers and poets. They are still favoured by today's intellectuals, but the magic has gone.

Tête-à-tête, boulevard St-Germain

to Parisians simply as La Madeleine. Two partly erected churches were successively razed before Napoleon had this temple built in honour of his Grande Armée. It was completed only in 1842, and by then it had been decided that the temple would be a church.

Fifty-two massive Corinthian columns surround the building, which dominates the centre of the place de la Madeleine with its flower market and well-known luxury delicatessens, Hédiard and Fauchon. Inside the church are some interesting 19th-century sculptures, including *Le Baptême du Christ* by François Rude, and *Le Mariage de la Vierge* by Pradier.
Place de la Madeleine, 75008.
Tel: 01 44 51 69 00. Open: daily 7.30am–7pm. Métro: Madeleine.

Les Deux Magots, a café frequented by post-war philosophers and poets such as Jean-Paul Sartre

Walk: St-Germain-des-Prés

Literary cafés, jazz cellars, informal bistros, bookshops, fashion boutiques, and antique shops, as well as one of the oldest churches in Paris, are the main attractions here. *Allow 2 hours.*

Start from the Odéon métro station.

1 Carrefour de l'Odéon

Cross over the boulevard St-Germain: No. 130 marks the entrance of the Cour du Commerce St-André. This alleyway and covered arcade has revolutionary associations: Marat's newspaper, *l'Ami du Peuple*, was printed at No. 8, and it was here that Dr Guillotin's deadly invention was first tested on sheep! On your right, enter the picturesque courtyards of the Cour de Rohan. *Retrace your steps and turn right.*

Relaxing by a floral forest

2 Rue de l'Ancienne Comédie

The most prestigious theatre company in France, the Comédie-Française, was performed at No. 14 until 1770. The Café Procope opposite has, since 1686, been the meeting place of writers, politicians, and philosophers *(see p104)*. *Follow rue Dauphine to the embankment, and turn left.*

3 Hôtel des Monnaies

This late 18th-century building, formerly the mint, houses the Musée de la Monnaie. Displays include medals, tools, presses, engravings, and drawings. *Tel: 01 40 46 55 35. Open: daily noon–5.30pm. Closed: Mon. Admission charge. Continue along quai de Conti to the place de l'Institut.*

4 Institut de France

The 17th-century domed building by Le Vau houses the Bibliothèque Mazarin, including Cardinal Mazarin's own collection of rare books. Since 1805, it has also housed the Institut de France, founded during the 1789 Revolution. It includes the Académie Française, set up by Richelieu in 1635. *Turn left into rue Bonaparte; on the right is the Ecole des Beaux Arts (Academy of Art), visible from the courtyard.*

5 Rues des Beaux-Arts, Visconti and Jacob

The whole area had many famous inhabitants including Oscar Wilde, Jean Racine, Honoré de Balzac, Eugène Delacroix, and Camille Corot. The rue de Seine is lined with art galleries, and rue Jacob has many antique shops and a couple of quiet hotels. Nearby is rue de Buci, with its well-known street market.
From rue Jacob turn right into rue de Fürstemberg.

6 Place de Fürstemberg

This charming little square seems to belong to another time and place: it looks delightfully provincial with its romantic catalpa trees and old-fashioned street lamps. Delacroix had his studio at No. 6; this is now a museum with mementoes of the artist.
*Open: daily 9am–5pm. Closed: Tue.
Rue de l'Abbaye brings you back to rue Bonaparte; turn left. The church of St-Germain des Prés was once part of a powerful abbey. Close by is the wide boulevard St-Germain.*

7 Literary Landmarks

Immediately on your right is the Café des Deux Magots and, almost next door, the Café de Flore, where intellectuals and artists have been meeting for generations. It is a good spot to get the feel of the area over a cup of coffee. The Brasserie Lipp opposite is a rather more select rendezvous for celebrities.
Continue up rue Bonaparte, then turn left into rue St-Sulpice. Pass the church and turn right along rue de Tournon.

8 Luxembourg

Marie de Médicis, widow of Henri IV, had the palace modelled on the Palazzo Pitti in Florence. It is now the seat of the Sénat. The gardens are adorned with numerous statues and the famous Fontaine de Médicis *(see p52)*.
Coming out of the gardens, follow rue Rotrou to the 18th-century place de l'Odéon. Rue Crébillon and rue Condé take you back to the Carrefour de l'Odéon.

Nearby
Rue St-André-des-Arts, Rue de Buci market.

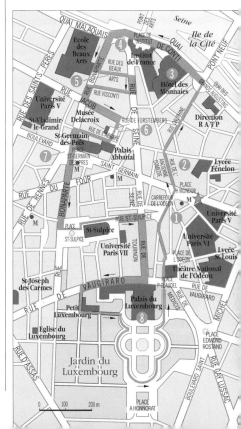

Streets and Squares

Elegant streets and popular ones, imposing squares and tiny, quaint ones, all reflect the life of the city, in turn quiet and bustling, hurried and leisurely.

The famous logo of a popular restaurant

Rue Mouffetard

Running downhill from the top of the Montagne Ste-Geneviève, the rue Mouffetard is one of the most picturesque streets in Paris. The bottom section is the liveliest, with its open-air market, the colourful shop signs creating a village-like atmosphere. A little way up, on either side, are the passage des Postes and the passage des Patriarches, both worth exploring, while further up still, on the left, the rue du Pot-de-Fer has some interesting restaurants. The Fontaine du Pot-de-Fer, on the corner, was built in the 17th century and supplied by an aqueduct that brought water to the Palais du Luxembourg. The street ends at the charming place de la Contrescarpe. *75005. Métro: Monge or Censier-Daubenton.*

Rue Quincampoix

Situated near the Centre Pompidou, this old street was the scene, in 1720, of a famous scandal involving the Scottish financier, John Law. He founded a bank, encouraged wild speculation, and the inevitable crash ruined thousands. There are some interesting old houses near the junction with rue des Lombards. *75004. Métro: Châtelet or Rambuteau.*

The lively, open-air market charms visitors to the rue Mouffetard

Rue Royale

This elegant street, which links the place de la Concorde and the Madeleine, has wide pavements lined with luxury shops.

Near the place de la Concorde, Maxim's is still one of the leading restaurants of the capital.
75008. Métro: Concorde or Madeleine.

Rue St-André-des-Arts

Going west towards St-Germain-des-Prés from the Latin Quarter, the rue St-André-des-Arts is popular with young people and tourists enjoying the incessant animation around the cafés, crêperies, snack bars, souvenir shops, and bookshops.

The Cour du Commerce St-André on the left is an 18th-century arcade lined with shops and cafés with picturesque old beams.
75006. Métro: St-Michel.

Place du Châtelet

This was extensively remodelled by Haussmann, who commissioned two theatres from the architect Davioud: the Théâtre du Châtelet, where musicals, operas and concerts are still regularly staged, and the Théâtre de la Ville, once the Théâtre Sarah Bernhardt, where the famous actress delighted Parisians with her inspired performances.
75001. Métro: Châtelet.

Place Emile-Goudeau

This unpretentious square, where the famous Bateau-Lavoir building (*see p78*) once stood, still possesses some of the old magic of Montmartre.
75018. Métro: Abbesses.

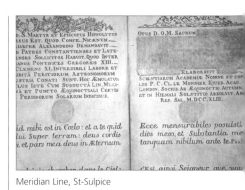

Meridian Line, St-Sulpice

Place de l'Odéon

The square has hardly altered since the late-18th century. The sober architecture of its houses contrasts with the Greek-temple style of the Théâtre National de l'Odéon dating from 1782. The Café Voltaire at No. 1 used to be the meeting place of 18th-century philosophers, including Voltaire, Diderot, and d'Alembert.
75006. Métro: Odéon.

Place St-Sulpice

Dominated by its monumental fountain (*see p53*) and the twin-towered church of St-Sulpice (*see p43*), this square is an ideal place for a pause while visiting the St-Germain-des-Prés area.
75006. Métro: St-Sulpice or Mabillon.

Place des Victoires

The original statue of Louis XIV was installed by a rich admirer of the king, who subsequently had the square designed by Mansart to match the statue. Recently renovated, the square has attracted several well-known fashion boutiques.
75002. Métro: Bourse or Palais-Royal.

VITAL STATISTICS

Total height: 320m.
First floor: 57m.
Second floor: 115m.
Third floor: 276m.
1,710 steps to the top.
Weight: 7,000 tonnes.
Maximum sway at the
top: 12cm. 40 tonnes of
paint are needed to
repaint it every seven
years. It has 4 million
visitors a year.

Tour Eiffel

Its spindly greyish figure has been painted, photographed, joked about, written and sung about more than any other monument in Paris, and today, after more than 100 years, the Eiffel Tower still retains the key to its initial success: instant appeal. Once your curiosity is roused, it will continue to grow as you get closer, and you will never be disappointed, for it is a strange monument indeed, with its graceful outline, combined with the huge steel struts that are locked together in an intricate web.

Scientific and Artistic Challenge
It is no surprise that the idea for such a daring project should have come from a

Once vilified on aesthetic grounds, now a favourite subject of artists

group of engineers, headed by Gustave Eiffel, working on steel bridges and viaducts. Plans submitted by Maurice Koechlin and Emile Nouguier won first prize in a competition organised for the 1889 Exposition Universelle, and Gustave Eiffel exclaimed enthusiastically: 'France will be the only nation with a 300m flagstaff!'

Built in Record Time
The tower was completed by 300 workers in just over two years from January 1887 to March 1889. This was made possible by the extreme precision of the plans, which gave the exact measurements for over 12,000 metallic parts. Two-and-a-half-million rivets were used and, when it was inaugurated, it was the tallest building in the world.

For and Against
The tower's success was immediate. During the six months of the exhibition, nearly 2 million visitors came to see the 'iron lady' and, by the end of the year, three-quarters of the building cost had

Queuing to climb the 1,710 steps to the top

already been recovered. The tower may have had its fans, but it also had its critics. Three hundred writers and artists signed a protest addressed to the municipality, qualifying it as 'useless and monstrous'.

A Narrow Escape

Concession had been granted to keep the structure standing for 20 years only, and the tower was due to be pulled down in 1909.

However, by then it was playing an essential role in the rapidly developing world of telecommunications. It was saved, and proved to be an indispensable asset in establishing the first radio telephone service across the Atlantic, and as a meteorological station. In 1957, its height increased by another 20m when a television transmitter was fitted at the top. In preparation for its hundredth anniversary, it was given a new look and completely repainted, and glitters elegantly now under more powerful lights.

The Climb!

A visit to the viewing platforms is a must. The view from the top floor is breathtaking, and can extend as far as 67km in exceptional weather conditions. If you wait until late afternoon on a clear day the sun has had time to disperse all signs of morning mist. Of course, you will most probably have to queue for the lifts, as the tower is very popular. On your way up, you may wish to stop on the first floor where there is a free video show on the history of the building.

Champ de Mars, 75007.
Tel: 01 44 11 23 23. www.tour-eiffel.Fr
Open: 9.30am–11pm (till midnight in summer). Admission charge.
Métro: Trocadéro or Bir-Hakeim.
RER: Champ-de-Mars-Tour-Eiffel.

Nearby
Jardins du Trocadéro, Palais de Chaillotand and its museums, Musée des Arts Asiatiques-Guimet, Musée d'Art Moderne de la Ville de Paris.

Unknown Paris

Paris is more than breathtaking vistas, impressive monuments, or glamour associated with the Champs-Elysées–Madeleine–Opéra districts. It can also be seen at a more leisurely pace along a canal, or in a hidden museum, in an arcade, or even in a cemetery.

Millions of skeletons lie in the Catacombs

Underground Paris

The city's network of tunnels has many practical uses other than the métro, and part of it can be visited. In the 18th century, Parisians found a new use for some underground galleries on the site of Roman stone quarries. They became a much-needed cemetery to relieve the overcrowded Cimetière des Innocents situated near les Halles, where the Fontaine des Innocents now stands. The site was consecrated, and the bones were piled along the galleries. There are now guided visits to these '**catacombs**'.

Les Catacombes, 1 place Denfert-Rochereau, 75014. Tel: 01 43 22 47 63. Open: 2–4pm, also 9–11am on Sat & Sun. Closed: Mon. Admission charge. Métro: Denfert-Rochereau.

Les Egouts (sewers) formed part of the modernisation programme of Baron Haussmann in the 19th century, the network totalling some 2,000km. The visit includes the showing of a video film which explains how the whole system works.

Place de la Résistance, 75007. Tel: 01 53 68 27 82. Open: 11am–4pm (5pm in summer). Closed: Thu & Fri. Admission charge. Métro: Alma-Marceau.

Along the Canal St-Martin

The Canal St-Martin was dug in the early 19th century to link the Canal de l'Ourcq, running eastwards from La Villette, and the Seine. It winds its way across the eastern districts of Paris over a distance of 4.5km and joins the river just south of the Bastille.

The most picturesque section lies between rue du Faubourg du Temple and rue Louis Blanc. The most relaxing way to enjoy the canal is to take a three-hour cruise from the Musée d'Orsay to La Villette. (*See* Organised Tours, *p186.*)

For those who prefer to walk beside the canal, the best way is to start either from the place de la République (métro République), or the place de Stalingrad (métro Stalingrad or Jaurès).

Arcades

Covered arcades were in fashion at the end of the 18th and at the beginning of the 19th century. Some of them, like the Galerie Vivienne (*see p97*), were elaborately decorated. Called *galeries* or *passages*, they are today lined with boutiques. The best are between rue de Rivoli and the Grands Boulevards, west of the boulevard de Sébastopol. The following should not be missed:

Galerie Vivienne *4 rue des Petits-Champs, 75002. Métro: Bourse.*
Passage Choiseul *23 rue St-Augustin, 75002. Métro: Quatre-Septembre.*
Passage des Princes *97 rue de Richelieu, 75002. Métro: Richelieu-Drouot.*
Passage des Panoramas *11 boulevard Montmartre, 75009. Métro: Montmartre.*
Passage Jouffroy *12 boulevard Montmartre, 75009. Métro: Montmartre.*
Passage Verdeau *31 bis rue du Faubourg-Montmartre, 75009. Métro: Le Peletier.*
Passage du Caire *2 place du Caire, 75002. Métro: Sentier.*
Galerie Véro-Dodat *19 rue Jean-Jacques Rousseau, 75001. Métro: Louvre-Rivoli.*

Cimetière du Père-Lachaise

This is Paris's largest cemetery. A plan is available at the main entrance to help you locate the graves of the famous: Alfred de Musset was buried beneath a weeping willow; the tragic lovers Héloïse and Abélard (*see p60*) are buried here; so are Oscar Wilde and Molière, Baron Haussmann, actress Sarah Bernhardt, singer Edith Piaf, and others.
Main entrance from the boulevard de Ménilmontant 75020.
Métro: Père-Lachaise.

On the east side of the cemetery is the old village of **Charonne**. Its medieval church of St-Germain-de-Charonne is surrounded by a tiny cemetery, and its high street, rue St-Blaise, is lined with small houses. The area has managed to retain its village atmosphere despite being close to the high-rise buildings of Belleville and Ménilmontant, north of the Père-Lachaise.
Métro: Gambetta.

Musée des Arts et Traditions Populaires

Situated in the Bois de Boulogne, this museum depicts aspects of French society through its traditions and daily life in rural areas, and includes folk art, local customs, and games.
6 avenue du Mahatma Gandhi, 75016.
Tel: 01 44 17 60 00. Open: 9.30am–5.15pm. Closed: Tue. Admission charge.
Métro: Les Sablons.

Musée Cernuschi

The house and personal collection of Oriental art of banker Henri Cernuschi form the basis of this museum, bequeathed to the city of Paris before his death in 1896. Ancient Chinese art, including Neolithic terracottas, is particularly well represented.
7 avenue Vélasquez, 75008.
Tel: 01 45 63 50 75. Open: 10am–5.40pm. Closed: Mon. Admission charge.
Métro: Monceau or Villiers.

Edith Piaf's tomb, Père-Lachaise cemetery

Musée des Lunettes et des Lorgnettes

The history of spectacles and various kinds of glasses, such as opera and fieldglasses, is depicted by means of many fascinating exhibits, sometimes elaborately decorated.

380 rue St Honoré, 75008. Tel: 01 40 20 06 98. Open: Tue–Sat 10am–noon, 3–6pm. Closed: Sun, Mon, & Aug. Métro: La Muette.

Musée Nissim de Camondo

This private mansion backing on to the Parc Monceau was donated to the nation by the Comte de Camondo. It recreates the interior of an elegant 18th-century house with furniture made by the most famous cabinetmakers, and with Beauvais tapestries, precious ornaments, and china.

63 rue Monceau, 75008. Tel: 01 53 89 06 40. Open: 10–5pm. Closed: Mon & Tue. Admission charge. Métro: Villiers or Monceau.

Musée Seita

This is an unusual museum depicting the development of smoking customs since Jean Nicot imported tobacco into France in the 16th century and unknowingly gave his name to one of its harmful ingredients, nicotine. Exhibits include pipes, snuff boxes, cigarette cases, and shop signs.

12 rue Surcouf, 75007. Tel: 01 45 56 60 17. Open: 11am–7pm. Closed: Sun. Admission charge. Métro: Invalides.

Nouvelle Athènes

Situated south of the place Pigalle, this district owes its romantic name partly

Elegant staircase at the Musée Gustave Moreau

to the Neo-Classical architecture of its houses, and partly to the fact that, in the early 18th century, it attracted the artistic and intellectual elite of the capital, and rivalled the Faubourg St-Germain.

Musée de la Vie Romantique

Housed in the former home of the painter Ary Scheffer, the museum is devoted to the artists and writers who used to be his regular guests: George Sand, Chopin, Delacroix, Liszt, Dickens, Turgenev, and many others.

16 rue Chaptal, 75009. Tel: 01 48 74 95 38. Open: 10am–5.40pm. Closed: Mon. Admission charge. Métro: St-Georges or Pigalle.

Musée Gustave Moreau

Another 19th-century painter's house has been turned into a museum. Moreau's symbolism influenced his famous pupils, Rouault and Matisse.

14 rue de la Rochefoucauld, 75009. Tel: 01 48 74 38 50. Open: Mon & Wed 11am–5.15pm, Thu–Sun 10am–12.45pm

& 2–5.15pm. Closed: Tue. Admission charge. Métro: Trinité or St-Georges.

Passy
Annexed to the city of Paris in 1860, the 'village' of Passy is today a much sought-after residential district in the western part of the capital.

Maison de Balzac
This museum is devoted to the 19th-century novelist who depicted French society with such mastery. It contains manuscripts, caricatures, and engravings. Balzac lived in the house for seven years and regularly evaded his creditors by slipping out through the back entrance in the cobbled rue Berton.
47 rue Raynouard, 75016. Tel: 01 42 24 56 38. Open: 10am–5.40pm. Closed: Mon. Admission charge. Métro: Passy. RER: Kennedy-Radio-France.

Musée du Vin
The museum has found an apt home in the ancient cellars of the 14th-century former Abbey of Passy; wine-tasting is included in the visit.
Rue des Eaux, 75016. Tel: 01 45 25 63 26. Open: 10am–6pm. Closed: Mon. Admission charge. Métro: Passy.

Temple
This district south of the place de la République was named after the Knights Templars. In 1808 the site was turned into an open-air second-hand clothes market known as the Carreau du Temple because the clothes were laid directly on the pavement. Today, cheap clothes are sold in a covered market, but the site has retained its picturesque name.
Métro: Temple.

Val-de-Grâce
The buildings of the former abbey are situated on the edge of the Latin Quarter. Mansart designed the church in the Jesuit style fashionable at that time, with a two-tier façade, a dome modelled on St Peter's in Rome and, above all, superb baroque decorations. Particularly remarkable are the huge baldachin resting on six twisted columns, and the painting in the cupola by Pierre Mignard. Following the Revolution, the abbey became a military hospital.
Rue St-Jacques (boulevard de Port-Royal end), 75005. RER: Port-Royal or Luxembourg.

Bacchus at the Musée du Vin

La Villette

The vast complex of La Villette has been developed on both sides of the canal de l'Ourcq, between the Porte de la Villette and the Porte de Pantin. Buildings on the original site have been incorporated into the project. The object of building a major new cultural centre on the edge of the city was to revive interest in this long-neglected eastern district, while taking advantage of the enormous amount of space that was available.

The futuristic design of the complex

Cité des Sciences et de l'Industrie

Inaugurated in 1986, the complex has already proved very successful, attracting an increasing number of visitors of all ages. Much more than a museum, it is a constantly updated reference centre, keeping track of the rapid evolution of science and technology. Its novelty lies in the fact that visitors are encouraged to take part in various projects and demonstrations. This makes it a realistic and entertaining study centre, particularly suitable for children.

The building itself, incorporating a former 19th-century auction hall, was designed by Fainsilber, who used the reflection of light off the steel-and-glass structure to achieve futuristic effects. The glass reveals mechanisms usually kept hidden, as in the main escalators or the glasshouses on the south façade.
30 avenue Corentin-Cariou, 75019. Tel: 01 40 05 12 12. Open: 10am–6pm (7pm on Sun). Closed: Mon. Admission charge; headsets for self-guided audio tour of Explora *in English can be rented. Métro: Porte-de-la-Villette or Corentin-Cariou.*

Explora

This permanent exhibition, staged on three levels and including tours, activities, and workshops, illustrates four broad themes:

The **Earth and the Universe** deals with the exploration of the oceans, the geological history of the earth, movements of the continents, travel, and experiments in space. The Planetarium aims to explain the complexity of the universe with programmes such as 'Life and Death of a Star' and 'Space Oasis'. **The Adventure of Life** deals with the human environment, man, and the secrets of life. **Man and Matter** is concerned with man's control of energy and other resources, transport, and economic trends. **Language and Communications** covers the world of sounds and images and various aspects of man's social behaviour.

The centre also includes a fully computerised, multi-media library with special material available for children (*la Médiathèque*), a cinema showing documentaries and fiction films to introduce viewers to the world of science *(le Cinéma Louis-Lumière)*, and two discovery areas for children aged 3 to 6 and 6 to 12 years *(l'Inventorium)*.

La Géode

This shiny steel globe, close to the main building, acts as a vast mirror, reflecting the surroundings and the changing sky with great intensity. The auditorium has a 1,000-sq m hemispheric screen. Films on scientific subjects are shown throughout the day.

The Maison de la Villette, housed in the recently renovated Rotonde des Vétérinaires, has an exhibition of local history. The park extends across the canal de l'Ourcq: green open spaces, with red *folies* (follies) dotted about. These are see-through cubical pavilions, varying in shape and used for practical purposes. There is a children's centre, information centre, video studios, café,

and first aid centre. The Grande Halle, dating from 1867, is an iron structure that was a cattle market until the 1970s. It is now a venue for exhibitions and trade fairs. The **Zénith** is a vast hall that has the capacity to accommodate approximately 6,500 spectators and is used mainly for rock concerts.

The **Cité de la Musique** is the other main complex in the park. It is the home of the Conservatoire National Supérieur de Musique, the higher national music academy, and houses a concert hall and the **Musée de la Musique**.

La Géode: film shows are every hour 10am–9pm. Admission charge.
Cité de la Musique: avenue Jean-Jaurès, 75019. Métro: Porte de Pantin.
Musée de la Musique: Open: noon–6pm (10am– 6pm Sun).
Closed: Mon. Admission charge.

The spectacular Géode is set in a landscaped park with good family facilities

Paris Environs

La Défense

This entirely modern district lies to the west of Paris, across the Pont de Neuilly. A statue in the central square, symbolising the defence of Paris during the Franco-Prussian war of 1871, gives the area its name.

Bold Town Planning

Town planners had been toying for a long time with the idea of extending the Voie Triomphale. This broad avenue designed by Le Nôtre in the 17th century, sweeps across the city in a straight line from the Louvre to the Arc de Triomphe.

Development began in the late 1950s, and architects experimented with new ideas. One of the driving principles was the total separation of pedestrian and motorised traffic. The vast complex is surrounded by a *boulevard circulaire* (ring road) carrying through-traffic, with underground link roads and outlets leading to specific areas at different levels.

A broad pedestrian avenue, called the Esplanade du Général de Gaulle, rises in steps from the Seine and gives access to the various groups of buildings: a variety of towers housing offices, a few blocks of flats, a vast shopping complex called Les Quatre-Temps, and the CNIT (Centre National des Industries et des Techniques), the oldest building on the site. Its concrete shell, resting on just three supports, was considered revolutionary in 1958! It has recently been converted into an international business centre.

La Grande Arche

Inaugurated in 1989 just in time for the bicentenary of the Revolution, La Grande Arche was the last project to be built. Designed by the Danish architect, Otto von Spreckelsen, the arch is shaped like a huge hollow cube, so vast that Notre-Dame (spire included) would fit beneath it! It is faced with glass and white Carrara marble, and is slightly out of alignment with the axis of the Voie Triomphale. The complex glass-and-steel structure of the external lifts offsets the extreme simplicity of the outline, and the *nuages* (clouds) suspended below the arch add a whimsical touch. The lifts take visitors up to the roof (le Belvédère) to admire the beautiful views over Paris.
3.5km west of the Porte Maillot. Métro & RER(A): Grande Arche de la Défense.

Malmaison

Situated 10km west of Paris, the elegant 17th-century Château de Malmaison is famous for its connection with Napoleon. His first wife, Joséphine de Beauharnais, bought the castle in 1799, and Napoleon always loved the place. When he divorced her in 1809 to marry Marie-Louise of Austria, Joséphine kept Malmaison for a short while until her premature death in 1814. Napoleon revisited the castle when he escaped from the island of Elba and returned to France, and again, just before he was finally exiled on the island of St Helena.

The castle had many owners before it was eventually donated to the nation and turned into a museum, housing

mementoes of Napoleon and Joséphine. Some of the original furniture from their various residences is on display.
Musée National du Château de Malmaison, avenue du Château, 92500 Rueil-Malmaison. Tel: 01 41 29 05 55. Open: 10am–noon, 1.30–4.30pm. Closed: Tue. Admission charge. RER: La Défense. Bus: 258 to Le Château.

The nearby **Château de Bois-Préau,** which also belonged to Joséphine, is devoted to mementoes of Napoleon's exile on the island of St Helena.
Avenue de l'Impératrice Joséphine, 92500 Rueil-Malmaison. Open: 10.30am–12.30pm, 1.30–5pm. Closed: Tue.

Sèvres

This small town, 10km west of Paris, has become synonymous with beautiful china. The Manufacture Nationale de Porcelaine began making fine porcelain here in the 18th century. Its specialities include the famous *bleu de Sèvres*, a deep blue on a pure white background, and exquisite *biscuits*, unglazed delicate statuettes.

Founded in 1824, the Musée National de la Céramique contains precious exhibits from all over the world.
Place de la Manufacture, 92310 Sèvres. Tel: 01 41 14 04 20. Open: 10am–5pm. Closed: Tue. Admission charge. Métro: Pont de Sèvres.

The cavernous Grande Arche de la Défense has a rooftop exhibition gallery

Baron Haussmann's Revolution

Just over 100 years ago, a revolution shook Paris to its very foundations and altered the city more drastically than 1789 had done. It was orchestrated by one man, Baron Haussmann, with the enthusiastic approval of Napoleon III. By 1850, the town had grown round its medieval centre without any coherence, and the squalid, narrow streets were a constant health hazard. Moreover, growing social problems threatened the fragile political stability.

From 1853 to 1870, Haussmann's engineers and architects cut right through the heart of the old city, laying waste whole districts, installing an adequate water supply and a network of sewers, creating wide avenues, and building rows and rows of six-storey blocks of flats which have become one of the familiar sights of the town.

Modern Paris emerged out of the chaos and soon became known as *la ville lumière*, a harmonious ensemble of green open spaces, including the Bois de Boulogne, of spacious, tree-lined boulevards, and imposing public buildings such as the Opéra.

Haussmann's far-seeing town planning was conceived on a scale that left room for expansion, and by the end of the century the railway stations, the Eiffel Tower, and the Grand and the Petit Palais had all taken their rightful place on the Paris scene.

The painful surgery Haussmann imposed on the capital was, however, much criticised at the time by such public figures as Victor Hugo, George Sand, and Alexandre Dumas who denounced the ruthless break with the past, and the crippling cost of these 'extravagant' schemes which encouraged speculation. But history has passed a more favourable judgement, for it was Haussmann who enabled Paris to blossom into the unique capital city it is today.

Georges Eugène Haussmann, town planner extraordinaire, whose vision created modern Paris –
with buildings like the Petit Palais (opposite), the Grand Palais (above) and the Opéra (below)

St-Denis

This industrialised northern suburb is famous for its beautiful Gothic cathedral, where most French monarchs have traditionally been buried.

The Legend of Saint-Denis

The first bishop of Paris, Saint-Denis, martyred in Montmartre, is said to have walked, holding his head in his hands, to a field where he died and was buried. His grave soon became a place of pilgrimage, and the first church was built there in the 5th century; then, in 630, King Dagobert founded a powerful abbey to control the growing numbers of pilgrims. He was buried in the new church, which became the traditional burial place of his successors.

The Gothic Church

Abbot Suger is closely linked to the history of the present cathedral. Born of poor parents, he was taken into care by the abbey. His exceptional gifts having won him the confidence of Louis VII, he became abbot of St-Denis in 1122 and designed a great Gothic cathedral which served as a prototype for later masterpieces such as Chartres Cathedral. The edifice was completed in just over 10 years. During the second half of the 13th century, Saint-Louis had the nave and transept rebuilt by Pierre de Montreuil, the architect of the Ste-Chapelle, but the beautiful façade remained unaltered.

Grossly neglected over the centuries, the cathedral suffered great damage during the 1789 Revolution. Restoration work carried out in the 19th century involved the pulling down of the north tower. Viollet-le-Duc, who also restored Notre-Dame, finally undertook to save what was left.

The Cathedral Today

The façade looks mutilated without its north tower. The base of the towers, over the rose window, is crenellated, a reminder that the edifice was originally fortified. The tympanum of the main portal illustrates the *Last Judgement*, the other two being connected with Saint-Denis.

The cathedral is, above all, a museum of the French monarchy, with its numerous funeral monuments carved by the greatest sculptors. In the 13th century, Saint-Louis commissioned monuments for his predecessors, the most remarkable being Dagobert's imposing tomb. It became the tradition for later kings to have their own grave designed. Some, dating from the Renaissance, are particularly elaborate, such as the monument commissioned by Catherine de Médicis for herself and Henri II.

In the Romanesque crypt is the collective grave of all the Bourbons.

Bearly friends at the Bois de Vincennes

Place de l'Hôtel de Ville, 93200
St-Denis. Tel: 01 48 09 83 54.
Open: 10am–5pm (7pm in summer).
Métro: St-Denis-Basilique.

Vincennes

The Château and Bois de Vincennes lie
just beyond the Périphérique, on the
eastern side of Paris.

The Château

Situated on the edge of what was once a
royal hunting ground, the Château de
Vincennes dates from the 14th century.
During the reign of Louis XIV, pavilions
were built on either side of the
courtyard overlooking the forest by the
architect Le Vau. By then the keep had
become a state prison, Fouquet and
Mirabeau being among its unwilling
guests. Extensive work has now restored
the castle as it was in the 17th century.

Near the entrance, the Tour du
Village, which formed part of the
fortified wall, is the only one to have
retained its original height of 42m. The
imposing keep, 52m high, is surrounded
by a separate wall and moat. It houses a
museum depicting the castle's history.
Avenue de Paris, 94300 Vincennes.
Tel: 01 43 28 15 48. Open: 10am–5pm
(6pm in summer). Admission charge.
Métro: Château de Vincennes.

The Bois de Vincennes

This has been known to generations of
French schoolchildren as the place
where Saint-Louis used to administer
justice seated under an oak tree. In 1860
Baron Haussmann remodelled it into an
English-style park, with a racecourse.
The **Parc Floral de Paris** and a **zoo** are

The Royal Chapel in the grounds of Vincennes

also situated here.
Parc Floral de Paris – route de la
Pyramide. Tel: 01 55 94 20 20.
www.parcfloraldeparis.com
Open: 9.30am–5pm (8pm in summer).
Admission charge.
Métro: Château de Vincennes.
Parc zoologique – avenue Daumesnil.
Open: 9am–5.30pm (6.30pm in summer).
Admission charge. Métro: Porte Dorée.

Musée des Arts d'Afrique et d'Océanie

Among the most interesting exhibits of
this museum is a collection of painted
bark from Australia, masks from Africa,
and fine samples of North African
crafts. There is also a tropical aquarium.
293 avenue Daumesnil, 75012. Tel: 01 44
74 84 80. Open: 10am–5.30pm.
Closed: Tue. Admission charge.
Métro: Porte Dorée.

Further Afield

CHANTILLY

Situated north of Paris on the edge of an ancient forest, in the heart of horse-racing country, the Château de Chantilly is surrounded by a beautiful park with ponds and lakes.

The Castle

The history of the castle goes back to Roman times: Cantilius was the first nobleman to build a fortified house on the site. In the 16th century the house was replaced by a castle with a splendid Renaissance edifice, and the Petit Château was built next to it. In 1662 Le Nôtre remodelled the gardens and park. One of Louis Philippe's sons, the Duc d'Aumale, rebuilt the Grand Château, damaged during the Revolution. On his death in 1897, he left the whole estate to the nation, including his magnificent art collections, which form the basis of the Condé museum.

The Museum

In the Petit Château are the former private apartments. The library contains the precious 15th-century illuminated manuscript of *Les Très Riches Heures du Duc de Berry*. In the chapel there is an altar carved by Jean Goujon, and 16th-century stained glass, and in the Grand Château there are paintings by Poussin, Corot, Raphael, Watteau, Ingres, and Botticelli, a unique collection of portraits by Clouet, father and son, and the famous Grand Condé diamond, stolen in 1926, but found later in an apple where it had been hidden by the thieves.

The Park

Most of Le Nôtre's masterpiece of landscape gardening remains: the grand canal and its waterfall, and the shorter canal lined with formal gardens leading to the raised terrace. The *hameau* (hamlet), added in the 18th century, is similar to the more famous one in Versailles. The Jardin

Château de Chantilly, full of treasures

Anglais (English garden) was designed in 1820.

The Grandes Ecuries

The vast stable was designed in the 18th century to house 250 horses, 500 dogs, and 100 attendants. It is now a museum. *The Prix du Jockey-Club-Lancia* and the *Prix de Diane-Hermès* are run every year in June on the beautiful racecourse in front of the stables.
35km north of Paris. Open: 10.30am–5.30pm. Closed: Tue. Admission charge.

CHARTRES

Chartres is the main town of the vast plain of La Beauce, 85km southwest of Paris. In the centre of the old town, on the left bank of the River Eure, stands one of the most beautiful cathedrals in France. Rebuilt in the space of 25 years after a fire destroyed part of the Romanesque edifice in 1194, spared by wars and revolutions, the cathedral is a unique example of French early-Gothic style showing remarkable architectural unity. Pilgrims have been flocking to Chartres since medieval times and, in 1935, students started their own pilgrimage, which takes place every year at the end of April.

The Façade

The originality of the façade stems from the contrast between the sombre outline of the Clocher Vieux on the right, in pure Romanesque style, and the rich decoration of the slightly taller spire of the Clocher Neuf, added in 1506. The Portail Royal, famous for its series of tall, column-like figures, and the three windows above it are 12th-century, the rest being 13th-century. The portals of the north and south transepts, dating from the 13th century, are equally remarkable.

The Interior

The proportions are vast, with an overall length of 130m and a height of 37m. The Gothic nave, the widest in France, appears relatively short in comparison with the transept and chancel. In the faint light, the deep, rich colours of the stained-glass windows, dating from the 12th and 13th centuries, immediately capture the attention. The elaborate choir-screen with its 41 groups of sculptures, depicting the life of Christ and the Virgin Mary, was designed in 1514 by Jehan de Beauce. The crypt is the largest in France and the oldest part of the cathedral. There are traces of a Gallo-Roman wall and a deep well.

The old town between the cathedral and the river has been renovated, and offers a pleasant journey back in time, especially along the rue des Ecuyers and adjacent streets.
Admission charge to the crypt and gallery of the Clocher Neuf.

Chartres Cathedral, a magnet for pilgrims

COURANCES

The Château de Courances is situated 55km south of Paris in wooded country. It is near the small town of Milly-la-Forêt, famous for its beautiful 15th-century covered market.

The original Renaissance castle was remodelled in the early 17th century into a fine example of Louis XIII style. The intricate design of the brick panels, accentuated by stone borders, is offset by the absence of decoration, while the steep slate roofs add an interesting contrast of colours. The outline of the strictly symmetrical edifice is enhanced by the softness of the green setting, reflected in the water of the moat and artificial lakes. A copy of the famous staircase at Fontainebleau was added in the 19th century. The castle is still inhabited and only open at weekends.

The gardens were planned by Le Nôtre, who gave a romantic aspect to his masterly design through the use of reflection in the water of several canals supplied by the nearby River Ecole. *Guided visits on weekend afternoons 2–6pm, from Apr–Oct. Tel: 01 64 98 41 18. Admission charge. This visit can be combined with that of the Château de Fontainebleau, 17km to the east.*

DAMPIERRE

About 36km southwest of Paris, Dampierre-en-Yvelines is a small community situated at the heart of the Parc Naturel Régional de la Haute Vallée de Chevreuse, a protected rural area. The castle stands out against the dark wooded setting of the vast park laid out by Le Nôtre.

The 16th-century castle, rebuilt in the late-17th century for Colbert's son-in-law, has been the property of the Luynes family ever since; it was restored during the first half of the 19th century. The elegant brick and stone façade is flanked by two arcaded buildings on either side.

The ground-floor reception rooms have Louis XIV and Louis XV wood panelling. On the first floor are the royal apartments, splendidly decorated to honour the monarchs who stayed at Dampierre on various occasions: Louis XIV, Louis XV, and Louis XVI. At the top of the monumental staircase, the large reception room decorated with murals by Ingres is most remarkable. A colourful floral garden occupies part of the park. *Château de Dampierre. Tel: 01 30 52 53 24. Open: every afternoon from Apr–mid-Oct. Admission charge.*

Handsomely proportioned Dampierre Castle

ECOUEN

Ecouen is a peaceful community in the green belt surrounding Paris. It is barely 20km north of the city and is famous for its Renaissance castle, which houses the Musée National de la Renaissance.

The castle was built in the early 16th century for Anne de Montmorency. Like Chantilly, Ecouen became the property of the Condé family from whom it was confiscated during the 1789 Revolution. It was later used by Napoleon as a school for the daughters of members of the Légion d'Honneur. The façade is adorned with columns and surmounted by dormer windows with carved pediments. It has recently been turned into a museum of Renaissance art to relieve the overcrowded Musée National du Moyen Age – Thermes de Cluny *(see p86)*.

Furniture, wood panels, tapestries, ceramics – 8,000 exhibits in all are displayed in 34 rooms, which have retained their original decoration whenever possible, in particular their painted mantelpieces. On the ground floor there is a superb collection of arms; on the first floor, the private apartments of Montmorency and his wife have some interesting furniture, while a fine 16th-century tapestry, 75m long, takes up the whole of one wing. On the second floor, there are numerous 16th- and 17th-century ceramic compositions, stained glass with religious motifs, painted wood panels, enamels, and so on.
Château d'Ecouen. Tel: 01 34 38 38 51. Open: 9.30am–12.45pm & 2–5.45pm. Admission charge.
This visit can be combined with an excursion to the Château de Chantilly.

Gardens at Claude Monet's house, Giverny

GIVERNY

This village, situated near the town of Vernon, 80km west of Paris, has strong links with Impressionism through one of the main exponents of the movement, the painter Claude Monet, who lived there from 1883 until his death in 1926. His house has been turned into a museum containing mementoes of the artist and the friends and colleagues who were his guests. The garden, which he designed himself, inspired many of his paintings, including the huge *Nymphéas* exhibited in the Musée de l'Orangerie *(see p90)*.
Maison de Claude Monet. Tel: 02 32 51 28 21. Open: Apr–Oct, daily except Mon 10am–6pm. Admission charge.

FONTAINEBLEAU

Set at the heart of a splendid forest, this peaceful residential town lives in the shadow of its beautiful palace. A spring in the middle of the forest determined the choice of Fontainebleau as the site of a royal castle as far back as the 12th century. François I transformed the austere medieval castle into a magnificent Renaissance residence, sparing no expense in decorating the new buildings which form the central part of the palace. Henri IV extended the palace.

Louis XIV, Louis XV, and Louis XVI contributed further to the decoration of the apartments. Spared by the Revolution, the palace continued to be used by kings and emperors until the end of the 19th century, when it was turned into a museum.

The Exterior

The buildings surround four courtyards. Access to the palace is through the main courtyard, or Cour du Cheval Blanc. At the end of the courtyard is the famous 'horseshoe' staircase, from which Napoleon made a very emotional farewell to his imperial guard before his departure to Elba in 1814. Beyond is the Cour de la Fontaine, backed by the Galerie François I. The Cour de la Fontaine overlooks the Etang des Carpes, a small carp pond with a charming pavilion in its centre. Le Nôtre's formal garden is on one side of the pond, and the Jardin Anglais (English-style garden) is on the other side. In the centre of the latter is the Fontaine Bliaud. The oldest part of the palace surrounds the Cour Ovale. A

Double horseshoe staircase, Fontainebleau

monumental entrance gives access to the Cour des Offices which is lined with outbuildings dating from 1609.

The Interior

The Grands Appartements (state apartments) on the first floor start with the Galerie François I, with its original Renaissance decoration of stucco and frescoes. The Escalier du Roi leads to the magnificent Salle de Bal (ballroom); the ceiling and chimney piece are particularly remarkable. On the other side of the Cour Ovale are the Appartements Royaux, the monarchs' private and official apartments, which include the Salon du Donjon, the only remaining part of the medieval castle, and the Salle du Trône, formerly the king's bedroom. In the emperor's official apartments is the famous Salon Rouge, where he abdicated in 1814.

The Petits Appartements on the ground floor were the private apartments of Napoleon and Joséphine,

and contain some splendid Empire furniture.
65km southeast of Paris. Entrance: place du Général de Gaulle. Tel: 01 60 71 50 70. Open: 9.30am–4.15pm. Closed: Mon & Tue. Admission charge.

ROYAUMONT

The Cistercian abbey of Royaumont, founded by Saint-Louis in 1228 and richly endowed by his successors, remained powerful until the Revolution. The church was then demolished, and the extensive abbey buildings turned into a cotton mill. Royaumont, now owned by a foundation, is the scene of regular cultural activities.

Very little remains of the church. Next to it, the cloister, which encloses a garden, is the largest of any Cistercian abbey in France. The long refectory, where Saint-Louis served the monks himself during his visits to the abbey, is a masterpiece of early Gothic architecture. In the kitchens, the impressive vaulted ceiling rests on massive columns with fine carved capitals.

30km north of Paris. Tel: 01 30 35 59 00. Open: daily. Admission charge. This excursion can be combined with a trip to Chantilly.

ST-GERMAIN-EN-LAYE

This important residential town, 18km west of Paris, has a history going back to the building of the first castle in the 12th century. The Renaissance castle, erected in 1539 by Pierre Chambiges on the same site, was later extended by Jules Hardouin-Mansart, and the park and gardens were designed by Le Nôtre, including a magnificent Grande Terrasse, 2.4km long.

In 1855, Napoleon III restored the castle to its original state and set up the **Musée des Antiquités Nationales.** The museum's archaeological collections cover France's past from the palaeolithic period to the Dark Ages, and include a reconstruction of the famous Salle des Taureaux at Lascaux.
Place du Château. Tel: 01 39 10 13 00. Museum open: 9am–5.15pm. Closed: Tue. Admission charge. RER: St-Germain-en-Laye.

Castle museum of St-Germain-en-Laye

THEME PARKS

This popular form of family entertainment is represented in the Paris region by Disneyland® Resort Paris, situated some 30km east of the capital in the countryside of Marne-la-Vallée, France Miniature (25km west), and the Parc Astérix (25km north).

Disneyland® Resort Paris

At the heart of Disneyland® Resort Paris is the theme Disneyland® Park – only part of a vast holiday resort covering

© Disney

nearly 2,000 hectares, one-fifth the size of Paris. Next to Disneyland® Park is the newly-opened Walt Disney Studios® Park, a behind-the-scenes world of film, television, and animation where you can see some of your favourite characters.

Disneyland® Park, with its five magical lands, is an amazing mixture of fantasy and adventure where you can meet with Mickey Mouse, fly with Dumbo, explore the Swiss Family Robinson's tree house, be propelled to the moon through Space Mountain, and return to ground to follow the tracks of Indiana Jones™ and the Temple of Peril: Backwards! The resort also has seven themed hotels, a golf course, and Disney® Village, which offers a whole range of restaurants and shops and plenty of entertainment for both day and night. The key word is enjoyment.
Marne-la-Vallée, Cedex 4. Tel: 01 60 30 60 30. www.disneylandparis.com
Open: all year; daily timings vary with the seasons. Admission charge.
RER: Chessy (end of the line).

France Miniature

This theme park will take you on a lightning journey across France, travelling from one region to the next in a few minutes. Two thousand models reduced 30 times, including 168 monuments, 20 typical villages, landscapes, and scenes of daily life, are spread over a vast relief map of France that covers 5 hectares.

There are shops selling crafts and other products from the regions of France, exhibitions, stands where you can sample regional cuisine, a picnic area, and two restaurants.

25 route du Mesnil, Elancourt.
Tel: 01 30 62 40 79/08 36 68 53 35.
www.franceminiature.com Open: Apr–15
Nov 10am–7pm (Sat till midnight); Jul &
Aug 10am–8pm. Admission charge.
RER: St-Quentin-en-Yvelines, then
shuttle service to the theme park.

Parc Astérix

The setting is France under Roman occupation 2,000 years ago, seen through the eyes of the characters created by Albert Uderzo for his series of *Astérix* comic strips, in which the intelligent and cunning Gauls constantly outwit the dumb Romans.

Astérix, the hero, is the brain behind the action, and Obelix, his fat devoted friend, lends him his muscle power, with Getafix the druid and many others. But there is more. Parc Astérix is an adventure park with many outdoor activities for the whole family; shops in Via Antiqua and rue de Paris, a medieval square with its crowd of jugglers and acrobats, and two restaurants.
60128 Plailly. Tel: 01 36 68 30 10.
Open: Apr–Oct 10am–6pm (Jul, Aug, &
weekends 9.30am– 8pm).
Admission charge. RER: Roissy, then
shuttle service to the park.

VAUX-LE-VICOMTE

Situated 51km southeast of Paris, the Château de Vaux-le-Vicomte is a masterpiece of 17th-century French architecture. Fouquet, Louis XIV's finance minister, had gathered a colossal fortune and decided to build a castle that would be a symbol of his success. In 1656 he commissioned the best artists of his time, and no expense was spared. An army of 18,000 workers slaved away at the construction of the castle which was completed in just five years, and Fouquet invited Louis XIV to a splendid reception that greatly surpassed those given at court. Dishes of solid gold crowned dozens of buffet tables set out in the garden, while jewel-studded elephants lined the alleys of orange trees, and Chinese fireworks were shot off from the ponds. The king was so annoyed that he had Fouquet – who had already fallen from favour – arrested a few days later. After a lengthy trial the ambitious minister was condemned to life imprisonment. The castle changed hands several times during the next 200 years until it was bought by a rich industrialist, whose family have since restored both house and gardens.

The main building stands on a raised terrace surrounded by a moat. On the ground floor, six reception rooms on either side of the oval Grand Salon (drawing room) overlook the magnificent gardens. The frescoes on the ceilings, depicting mythological scenes, are by Le Brun. A staircase in the entrance hall gives access to the first-floor private apartments. From the terrace, the view sweeps across the gardens, which extend a long way on different levels, and are adorned with ornamental ponds, cascades, and a Grand Canal. In the stables there is a museum of horse-drawn carriages.
Vaux-le-Vicomte, 77950 Maincy, near
Melun. Tel: 01 64 14 41 90. Open: mid-
Feb–Mar 11am–5pm, Apr–Oct
10am–6pm. Admission charge.
Saturday candlelit visits from May–Sep
8.30–11pm. There is a cafeteria.

Versailles

For most people, Versailles is the supreme example of an aspect of French culture that blends elegance and refinement with a search for perfection, and that is sometimes coupled with excessive formality and bold confidence.

The beautifully detailed château

A Most Ambitious Project

In 1661, Louis XIV, the Sun King, decided to build a castle that would outshine Vaux-le-Vicomte (see p131) on the site of the modest brick and stone château built by Philibert Le Roy for his father in 1631.

For nearly 50 years the greatest artists worked at Versailles: the architect Le Vau, succeeded by Hardouin-Mansart; Le Brun, who supervised the interior decoration; and Le Nôtre, who surpassed himself in the design of the magnificent gardens. The King and his court moved in during 1682 – a total of 3,000 people, attending sumptuous receptions! From 1682 to 1789, Versailles was also the political centre of France.

During the Revolution, the furniture was sold, and the château gradually fell into disrepair until, in 1837, Louis-Philippe had it converted into a museum of French history.

After World War I, a complete restoration of the castle was undertaken with the financial help of JD Rockefeller, and Versailles has slowly regained its 18th-century elegance.

The Château

The approach to the château, one of the most visited monuments in France, is very impressive. There are a succession of three open courtyards to be traversed, the Court of Ministers, the Royal Court, and the Court of Marble, and Louis XIV's statue in the centre.

On the garden side, the 680-m long façade has a projecting central section. An elegant balustrade emphasises the roof line, and groups of elegant columns at regular intervals attract the eye as focal points.

State Apartments

On the way to the State Apartments, it is possible to have a look at the chapel, designed by Hardouin-Mansart but only completed after his death in 1710. The State Apartments include a suite of reception rooms, decorated with marble and paintings depicting mythological scenes; they were used for the entertainment of the court during the winter season.

The large windows of the 75-m long Galerie des Glaces (Hall of Mirrors), the most famous room in the palace, overlooking the gardens, let in the setting sun which reflects on the huge mirrors (not the original glass) covering the walls.

Next come the Queen's Apartments, in particular the Queen's bedroom where Louis XV and many royal children were born – in public. The King's Apartments are in Louis XIII's castle. The bedroom, remodelled by Louis XIV, was used by his successors until 1789. Next door is the Chambre du Conseil (Council Chamber), where political decisions were taken.

Château de Versailles, place d'Armes. Tel: 01 30 83 77 88. Open: daily except Mon. Admission charge. Free parking. RER: Versailles-Rive gauche. Château

open: 9am– 5.30pm (6.30pm in summer). Park open: 7am–dusk daily. Visits – without guide: Chapel & State Apartments: from entrance A on the right. With guide: Appartement du Roi, last visit starts at 4pm. Appartements du Dauphin et de la Dauphine et de Mesdames: guided visits during daylight hours. Events: every Sun from May to Oct the numerous fountains are turned on at 3.30pm. Combined fountains and firework displays are also held on some Saturday nights in summer.

Versailles

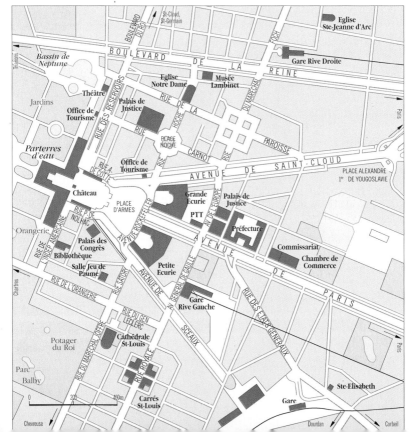

Cabinets Intérieurs du Roi

The King's private apartments, designed by Gabriel for Louis XV, include the bedroom where the King died in 1774, the games room, the study with its original desk, the music room, which Louis XV furnished for his favourite daughter, Madame Adélaïde and where the young Wolfgang Mozart is supposed to have played in 1763, and the beautiful library.

The **Cabinets Intérieurs de la Reine** were private apartments originally designed for Louix XV's queen, and were later refurbished for Marie Antoinette.

Opéra Royal

Built by Gabriel, the opera house was inaugurated in 1770 for the wedding of Marie Antoinette to the future Louis XVI. It could seat 700 spectators and

Versailles – Le Parc

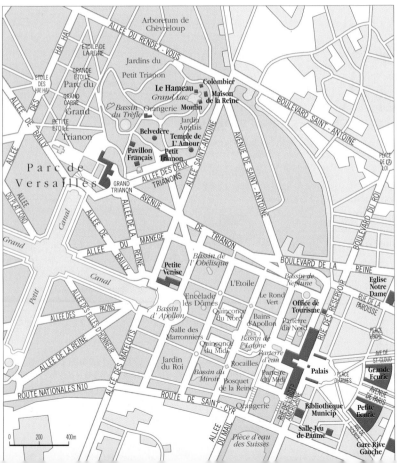

Waterways and fountains in the gardens at Versailles

could also be used as a grand reception room or a ballroom. On the ground floor are the recently renovated Appartements du Dauphin et de la Dauphine (the heirs to the throne), and those of Louis XV's daughters.

The Gardens

From the raised terrace in front of the château, the Grand Canal offers a magnificent vista which extends to the woods in the distance. The design of the gardens by Le Nôtre, between 1661 and 1668, is a masterpiece of geometry: the canal is the focal point of a composition on different levels, of ornamental ponds adorned with fountains, flower beds, bowers, and over 200 sculptures.

The Trianons

The Trianons are lesser palaces. The Grand Trianon, faced with pink marble, was built by Hardouin-Mansart for Louis XIV, who wished to give private receptions for Madame de Maintenon.

The Petit Trianon was commissioned by Louis XV and given by Louis XVI to Marie Antoinette who used it to be alone with her children. She had the garden completely remodelled and the charming *hameau* (hamlet) built nearby. *Cabinets Intérieurs de la Reine: guided tours: 9am–5.30pm (6.30pm in summer). Opéra Royal: last guided visit starts 4pm. Grand and Petit Trianons open: noon–5.30pm (6.30pm in summer). Entrance A on the right.*

Gardens and Greenery

A large city can become oppressive after a while, and you may suddenly feel the need to get away from the crowds and the incessant noise, particularly with the arrival of warm, sunny weather in late spring or summer. Paris and the Ile-de-France offer plenty of opportunities for a change of pace and scenery, in parks and floral gardens, in forests teeming with wildlife, and along quiet rivers.

The Bois: a slice of the countryside in the city

Bois de Boulogne

This favourite haunt of nature-loving Parisians, covering about 850 hectares, is crowded at weekends, but offers peace and quiet to those who wander off the beaten track along its shady avenues (take care after dusk). Many family activities are available: boating on the lakes, cycling along specially designed lanes, horse riding, and fishing. The **Jardin d'Acclimatation**, on the northern edge of the 'Bois', is a comprehensive amusement park for children *(see p159)*; nearby is the **Musée des Arts et Traditions Populaires** *(see p113)*, and there are clearly marked picnic areas.

This former royal hunting forest used to abound with deer, bear, and wild boar until Louis XV opened it to the public and it became fashionable. Given to the city of Paris in 1852 by Napoleon III, it was remodelled into an English-style park by Baron Haussmann, who created lakes, ponds, and the Longchamp racecourse. The Auteuil racecourse was built after the Franco-Prussian War in 1870, and at the turn of the 20th century fashionable horse-drawn carriages could be seen driving along the wide avenues that nowadays carry fast traffic bound for the *banlieue* (suburbs) just across the Seine.

In the northwest corner of the 'Bois' is the **Parc de Bagatelle,** a beautiful garden well known for its spring display of tulips and irises, and roses and water lilies in summer. The nearby **Jardins de Bagatelle** is an expensive restaurant in a lovely setting.

The **Pré Catelan**, in the centre of the Bois de Boulogne, is another attractive park with a magnificent 200-year-old copper beech; next to it, the **Jardin Shakespeare**, planted with flowers and trees mentioned in Shakespeare's plays, has a charming open-air theatre.
Entry from the north side.
Métro: Les Sablons. Bagatelle métro: Pont-de-Neuilly then No. 43 bus to place de Bagatelle; east side, RER: Avenue-Henri-Martin; south side, métro: Porte d'Auteuil. Bicycle rental available at the lakes; horse riding at the Centre Hippique, route de la Muette à Neuilly. Tel: 01 45 01 20 06.

Bois de Vincennes

See p123.

Jardin Albert-Khan

Situated just south of the Bois de Boulogne, this succession of gardens, created by the banker Albert-Khan, illustrates landscapes from different regions of the world: the forest of Vosges, a Japanese garden, an English garden, as well as a picturesque rock setting. The display of hundreds of flowers is at its best in late spring.

1 rue des Abondances, 92100 Boulogne. Open: 11am–6pm. Admission charge. Métro: Pont-de-St-Cloud, then bus No. 72, 52, or 175.

Jardin Fleuriste de la Ville de Paris

Plants used for decorating public buildings and for official occasions are grown in the greenhouses surrounding this municipal garden.

The huge tropical house contains palm trees, banana trees, and a host of tropical plants. Rare species are housed in a number of hothouses on the south side of the garden.

3 avenue de la Porte d'Auteuil, 75016. Open: daily 10am–5pm (6pm in summer). Admission charge. Métro: Porte d'Auteuil.

Orangerie, Parc de Bagatelle, the 'Bois'

Rising in the Langres plateau just northwest of Dijon and discharging into the English Channel, the Seine has played a vital role in the birth and development of the city of Paris.

The first settlers to occupy the area were fishermen, and for hundreds of years the river provided food, water, and protection to the people who lived on the Ile-de-la-Cité. When commerce became essential to the survival of the rapidly developing city, the Seine (the third-longest river in France) was the obvious means of communication, and proved quite lucrative for those who levied substantial tolls.

Because the economy of Paris depended on the river, it was natural that those who sought to rule the city should also seek to control its main port which, in medieval times was La Grève (now the place de l'Hôtel de Ville). In the 13th century, the guild of merchants obtained from the king the right to levy taxes from ships bringing in essential goods such as salt, wine, and wood. The harbour developed rapidly, and

today Paris is the main river port, and the fourth most important harbour in France.

The Seine has contributed much to their prosperity, and Parisians really love their river. They have built their most prestigious monuments along its banks, adorned it with beautiful bridges, and lined its embankment with trees to provide shade so that they can stroll there after a day's work or sit on one of the benches and relax in the cool of the evening.

The river's sometimes erratic behaviour can now be controlled, but memorable floods have been recorded in the past. Even today, whenever the river rises above its normal level, people flock eagerly to the Pont de l'Alma to see how much of the famous Zouave is under water.

Facing page: Zouave keeps a watchful eye on the water level at Pont de l'Alma; below: a working barge glides through Arsenal Basin; bottom: excursions on the Bateaux Mouches

Jardin des Plantes

Founded in 1626, the botanical gardens were greatly extended by the famous 18th-century naturalist, Buffon, and the menagerie was created during the Revolution. The Musée d'Histoire Naturelle (Museum of Natural History) houses departments of botany, mineralogy, palaeontology, and entomology.The gardens include the Jardin Alpin with 2,000 species of plants from mountainous regions from the Alps to the Himalayas; the Jardin d'Hiver housing heavy-scented tropical plants and flowers; a number of hothouses; a maze; and a herb garden devoted to medicinal plants.

Entrance from rue Cuvier, rue Buffon and Place Valhubert, 75005.
Tel: 01 40 79 30 00. Gardens, menagerie, museum, and maze open daily 7.30am–5.30pm (8pm in summer).
Free admission.
Métro: Gare d'Austerlitz.

Parc des Buttes-Chaumont

Situated in the 19th *arrondissement*, east of the centre, this park was landscaped by Haussmann on hilly wasteland. From the small temple, romantically set on the island in the middle of the lake, the view extends to the Butte Montmartre.
Métro: Buttes-Chaumont.

Parc Georges Brassens

Two bronze bulls at the main entrance are a reminder that the park was created on the site of the former Vaugirard slaughterhouses. A small garden filled with scented plants was specially designed for blind people, and the vineyard is the scene of festivities during the grape harvest in October.
Rue des Morillons, 75015.
Métro: Convention.

Parc Monceau

Situated in a fashionable residential area, close to the Arc de Triomphe, the

The delightfully landscaped Parc Monceau

Parc Monceau was landscaped as an English garden, with rocks and an oddly shaped lake, and adorned with mock ruins, pyramids, and statues following the Neo-Classical style fashionable in the 18th century.
Boulevard de Courcelles.
Métro: Monceau.

Parc Montsouris
Another of Haussmann's creations, this hilly park facing the Cité Universitaire (the student halls of residence) includes a large lake, waterfalls, a meteorological observatory, and a reproduction of the Bardo, the Bey of Tunis' palace.
Boulevard Jourdan.
RER: Cité-Universitaire.

Parc de St-Cloud
Situated in one of the elegant western suburbs overlooking the Seine, this park was designed by Le Nôtre. The castle, where Napoleon stayed many times, was destroyed by fire in 1870. The Grande Cascade, with its statues featuring the Seine and the Marne rivers, is particularly remarkable; so is the view across Paris from the terrace. The woods in the upper part of the park offer lovely cool walks in summer.
On the N186, 11km west of Paris.

Out of Town
The green belt round Paris includes several woodland areas, the largest being the Forêt de Rambouillet and the Forêt de Fontainebleau. There are also many rivers that wind their way towards the Seine along picturesque valleys such as the Vallée de Chevreuse with its quiet, twisting roads, and the ideal means to achieve complete relaxation is to join a leisurely cruise along the Seine for a few hours, or even a whole day.

Forêt de Fontainebleau
This vast forest surrounding the castle and town of Fontainebleau over an area of 25,000 hectares offers a landscape of wooded hills and valleys, of moors covered with heather and gorse, and of large rocks piled high in places. Pines, oaks, and beeches make up the majority of the forest. There are opportunities for rock climbing, and the area has become popular with amateurs and professionals.

Various itineraries are suggested in the *Guide des sentiers de promenades dans le Massif forestier de Fontainebleau,* available from the tourist office in Fontainebleau. Most tours start from the town. To the west are the Gorges de Franchard, a narrow glen scattered with impressive overhanging rocks. To the south, Le Long Rocher is a rock-strewn plateau that affords lovely views over the forest.
60km southeast of Paris.

Spend the day in Fontainebleau forest

Forêt de Rambouillet

Although less spectacular than Fontainebleau, this forest, covering 20,000 hectares, offers pleasant walks and cycle tours through ancient villages, along narrow rivers, and beside picturesque lakes. Oak and pine predominate, red deer and wild boar are plentiful, if not always easy to detect.

In the isolated northern part of the forest, fishermen seek peace and quiet on the shores of the Etang Neuf, near the solitary 16th-century castle of La Mormaire and the almost deserted village of Gambaiseuil. Further south, from the Rochers d'Angennes, a rock formation on high ground, there is a good view of the Etang d'Angennes, overgrown with reeds, and the secluded valley of the Guesle river.

L'Haÿ-les-Roses

Situated in the densely populated southern suburbs, halfway between Paris and Orly Airport, the rose garden of l'Haÿ-les-Roses was created 100 years ago; thousands of roses, wild, as well as hybrids, offer a grand display of colours in a charming setting framed with climbers. There is also a Musée de la Rose devoted to works of art connected with this aristocratic flower: prints, embroidery, ceramics, and small objets d'art.
8km south of Paris.

Parc de Sceaux

The gardens were designed by Le Nôtre, and Louis XIV was invited to a splendid reception to mark the inauguration of the castle, built in 1670. During the Revolution, the estate was bought for the use of the land and the castle was demolished. The state acquired the property in 1923, and undertook its restoration.

Once more, water is the focal point of the beautiful gardens: on the south side, a wide avenue leads to the Grandes Cascades, a succession of waterfalls supplying an octagonal lake surrounded by plane trees reflected in the still water; the grand canal is also lined with trees, which create contrasts of sunlight and shade, and temper the formal aspect of French-style gardens.

The Petit Château and the Pavillon de l'Aurore (in the northeast corner of the

WILDLIFE

You do not have to be a connoisseur to appreciate the subtle blend of colours and the fresh scent of woodland flowers in springtime. In the verdant Forêt de Fontainebleau, hyacinths, daffodils, and laburnum herald the return of warm weather, followed by hawthorn blossoms and fragile lilies-of-the-valley. Later on, dense bushes of gorse light up the green undergrowth, eclipsing the more discreet heather, campanulas and wild carnations. Summer offers the pleasure of looking for wild strawberries and raspberries, while autumn brings hazelnuts and chestnuts. These traditional hunting grounds still abound with roe deer and boar, as well as the more common foxes, hare and squirrels. There is also a great variety of birdlife, including the famous Fontainebleau woodpeckers.

park) date from the 17th century. In the latter there is an audio-visual presentation of the estate.
10km southwest of Paris.

Vallée de Chevreuse

The upper valley of the River Yvette is known as the Vallée de Chevreuse after the small town dominated by the ruins of its castle. In 1984, a regional park was created to preserve this area of natural beauty, consisting of woodland, lush meadows, and cultivated land. The D58, which follows the river westwards, leads to the Château de Dampierre *(see p126)*. To the north are the ruins of the Cistercian abbey of Port-Royal-des-Champs, famous in the 17th century for its criticism of the Jesuits. The southern road (D24) leads to Les Vaux de Cernay, where a picturesque stream makes its way through woods and rocks.
The town of Chevreuse is situated 30km southwest of Paris.

Walk or cycle in the Forêt de Rambouillet

Shopping

Part of the fun of staying in Paris is the opportunity to go on a shopping spree. Deciding where to go, however, can be quite bewildering in any large city, and particularly in Paris, where attractive shop windows are to be found round every street corner.

Paris is famous for its designer outlets

Before you embark on a shopping tour of Paris there are a few facts you should be aware of.

It is dangerous to carry large amounts of cash, as pickpockets frequent crowded places. The safest and most widely used method of payment in boutiques, department stores, and shopping centres is by credit card; but bear in mind that a minimum purchase of 15 Euro is required. Be prepared to pay cash at market stalls and food kiosks.

Tax-free shopping is now common practice for non-EU residents. Look out for the symbol on shop windows. You need to spend a minimum of 183 Euro to qualify for a tax refund. You will then be given a special bill in two parts; the shopkeeper will tell you where to send one of the copies for a VAT refund once it has been stamped by Customs.

Although shops remain open quite late in the evening *(see pp185–6),*

Village-style shopping, rue Mouffetard

individual shops are often closed on Monday morning, sometimes all day Monday. So, if planning a long weekend in Paris, it is better to opt for Friday rather than Monday.

Department Stores

All the large department stores except one are situated on the Right Bank. Moreover, Parisians often refer to the St-Lazare-Opéra district as the quartier des *grands magasins*, as the most prestigious of them are lined up along the boulevard Haussmann.

The **Galeries Lafayette** (40 boulevard Haussmann, 75009, *tel: 01 42 82 34 56*, métro Chaussée d'Antin), and **Le Printemps** (64 boulevard Haussmann, *tel: 01 42 82 50 00*, métro Havre-Caumartin), both established in the late-19th century, tend to lay emphasis more and more on elegance and fashion trends in clothes and accessories, as well as household goods. Their extensive ready-to-wear departments have attracted all the main designers. Le Printemps has devoted a separate building to menswear (Brummell).

Two other department stores situated between the Louvre and the Hôtel de Ville, along the rue de Rivoli, are less fashion-conscious and mainly sought after for their household goods. **The Bazar de l'Hôtel de Ville,** known as the BHV (52 rue de Rivoli, 75004, *tel: 01 42 74 90 00*, métro Hôtel de Ville), has an incredibly well-stocked DIY department in the basement. Nearby, **La Samaritaine** (19 rue de la Monnaie, 75001, *tel: 01 40 41 20 20*, métro Pont-Neuf) attracts a similar clientele, and you can enjoy a cup of tea on the roof

Galeries Lafayette: shop till you drop

terrace while admiring the splendid view over Paris.

Le Bon Marché (22 rue de Sèvres, 75007, *tel: 01 44 39 80 00*, métro Sèvres-Babylone) is the only department store on the Left Bank. It is rightly famous for its fine food section, **l'Epicerie**, which is open longer hours than the store itself.

Arcades

Quaint, old-fashioned, and full of atmosphere, some of these arcades make a change from traditional shopping (*see pp112–13*).

Always appealing, fresh produce at keen prices in a Montparnasse street market

Open-air Markets

These are the most ancient type of markets, but they have, for some time, been in fierce competition with the large supermarkets to supply Parisian households with fresh food. However, this is one battle the big stores are not about to win, for not only do open-air markets offer their demanding customers good quality and low prices, but they are also the very fibre of a district's social life – a meeting place where neighbours of different backgrounds exchange opinions.

Some of these markets are organised by the municipality, and usually take place on two or three mornings a week on a square or large open space. Canopied stalls are put up the night before, and early in the morning stallholders park their vans all around, usually creating huge traffic jams. They come straight from the central food market at Rungis, and their prices are very competitive indeed. Two such markets can be found in the Latin Quarter on the place Monge (métro Monge), and the place Maubert (métro Maubert-Mutualité).

Street markets usually run on a slightly different principle. Shops that sell fresh food in a particular street set up stands outside their premises on every day of the week except one, and advertise special offers. These markets are open until early evening to enable working people to get their daily supply of fresh vegetables on their way home. The rue Mouffetard (métro Censier-Daubenton) and the rue de Buci (métro Mabillon) markets in the Latin Quarter are among the best in Paris; the rue Lepic in Montmartre (métro Blanche) is also very attractive and lively.

Covered Markets

Steeped in tradition, these are the direct descendants of medieval structures known as *halles*, which usually consisted of a solid roof resting on large wooden pillars. Today, they are housed in proper buildings belonging to the municipality. They have cubicles all round, and fixed stalls in the centre where carefully selected shopkeepers offer good service in a friendly atmosphere. There are 13 covered markets in Paris, all to be found on the Right Bank, except one, which is situated in the rue Mabillon in St-Germain-des-Prés (métro Mabillon). Another interesting market is in the rue Lebon, near the place des Ternes, in the 17th *arrondissement* (métro Ternes).

Specialised Markets

The loveliest flower market in Paris is situated on the place Louis-Lépine, on the northern side of the Ile-de-la-Cité (métro Cité every day from 8am to 7pm, except on Sunday when it is replaced by a bird market. Another is held on the place de la Madeleine (métro Madeleine). There is also a small pet market along the quai de la Mégisserie on the Right Bank (métro Châtelet or Pont-Neuf).

On the corner of the avenue de Marigny and the avenue Gabriel (métro Champs-Elysées-Clémenceau), an extensive stamp market takes place on Thursday, Saturday, and Sunday.

Cheap new and second-hand clothes are sold in a covered market every morning except Monday on the Carreau du Temple (métro Temple).

Flea Markets

The most famous flea market in Paris is the Marchés aux Puces of the Porte de Clignancourt, in St-Ouen, which takes place on Saturday, Sunday, and Monday between 7.30am and 7pm, though bargains are very rare these days. Other, similar but more genuine, markets are held in the open, on Saturday and Sunday along the avenues Georges-Lafenestre and Marc-Sangnier (métro Porte de Vanves), and avenue de la Porte de Montreuil (métro Porte de Montreuil).

Shopping Centres

In some places a wide variety of boutiques are gathered under one roof for convenience.

The Forum des Halles, rue Pierre Lescot (métro Les Halles, *see pp54–5*), is an underground complex with shops of all sizes selling just about everything from *foie gras* to shoes. The Galeries des Champs Elysées, on the north side of

the famous avenue between the Rond-Point and the rue de Berri (métro Franklin-Roosevelt), are worth exploring for their elegant boutiques, as is the vast shopping complex at La Défense, Les Quatre-Temps, which has a network of lanes lined with shops on several levels, and a huge hypermarket called **Auchan.**

Specialised Streets and Areas

In the 9th *arrondissement* there are busy shopping streets north of the boulevard Haussmann, with a number of stamp collectors, high-class confectioners, up-market decorators, and fashion boutiques. Not far from there, in the 8th *arrondissement*, the area round the place de l'Europe is well known for its musical instrument makers and dealers.

On the place de la Madeleine can be found the finest high-class grocers and delicatessens in Paris: **Fauchon** and **Hédiard.**

South of the boulevard Haussmann, the avenue Matignon and rue du Faubourg St-Honoré are famous for their art galleries, while the avenue Montaigne and rue François I are the headquarters of fashion designers; the

Assessing a find in the stamp market

rue de la Paix and place Vendôme are lined with exclusive jewellers. The main glass and china manufacturers have their showrooms along the rue de Paradis, near the Gare de l'Est in the 10th *arrondissement*.

Trade Exhibitions

The Chambre de Commerce et d'Industrie de Paris *(tel: 01 55 65 66 00)* and Foires et Salons de France (*tel: 01 53 90 20 00)* publish a comprehensive list of trade exhibitions in Paris. The following is a selection.

Brocante de Paris: antiques fair in early February at the Espace Champerret, Porte de Champerret, 75017. *Métro: Louise-Michel.*

Foire à la Ferraille de Paris: literally a 'scrap-iron fair', in fact an antiques fair held in February, May, and September in the Parc Floral de Paris, Bois de Vincennes, 75012. *Métro: Château de Vincennes.*

Musicora: this international exhibition of classical music is held during April in the Grand Palais, avenue Winston Churchill, 75008. *Métro: Champs-Elysées-Clémenceau.*

Foire Internationale de Paris: includes tourism, books, gardens, wines, sports, and entertainment; held in May at the Parc des Expositions de Paris, Porte de Versailles, 75015. *Métro: Porte de Versailles.*

Mondial de l'Automobile: motor car show held every other year in October at the Parc des Expositions de Paris.

Salon du Cheval et du Poney: all about horses, with various activities and show jumping, held in December at the Parc des Expositions de Paris.

Antiques – worth a glance, browse, or buy

Salon Nautique International: popular boat show, held just before Christmas at the Parc des Expositions de Paris.

Where to Shop
Antiques
Le Louvre des Antiquaires
250 shops offer plenty of choice from French furniture to jewellery. *2 place du Palais-Royal, opposite the Louvre. Tel: 01 42 97 27 00. Métro: Palais-Royal.*

Carré Rive Gauche
Next to the Musée d'Orsay; formed by the Quai Voltaire, rue des St-Pères, rue de l'Université and rue du Bac. Métro: rue du Bac.

The Village Suisse
Over 100 dealers sell good-quality ornaments and furniture. *78 avenue de Suffre. Tel: 01 43 06 69 90. Métro: La Motte-Picquet-Grenelle.*

Drouot
Famous auctioneers. Salerooms at: *9 rue Drouot. Tel: 01 48 00 20 20. Métro: Richelieu-Drouot & Le Petetier. 15 avenue Montaigne. Tel: 01 48 00 20 80. Métro: Alma-Marceau.*

Over 50 antique dealers are established in the tiny pedestrian streets of the **Village St-Paul** in the Marais, (métro St-Paul or Pont-Marie). You can buy old prints and postcards from the booksellers on the quais along the Seine.

Books

The largest bookshops in Paris are the book departments of the:
FNAC stores in *boulevard St-Germain, Forum des Halles,* and *avenue des Ternes.* The 6th *arrondissement,* in and around the boulevard St-Germain, has many traditional bookshops.

Books in English are available from:
WH Smith
248 rue de Rivoli. Tel: 01 44 77 88 99. Métro: Concorde.

Galignani
A well-stocked, old-fashioned bookshop, with bilingual service.
224 rue de Rivoli. Tel: 01 42 60 76 07. Métro: Concorde.

Brentano's
37 avenue de l'Opéra. Tel: 01 42 61 52 50. Métro Opéra.

Village Voice
6 rue Princesse. Tel: 01 46 33 36 47.

Clothes

Apart from the exclusive fashion designers in the 8th *arrondissement,* there are trendy fashion boutiques in the area round the church of St-Germain des Prés, while department stores have a choice of more traditional wear. Bargains can be found in the avenue de Clichy in the 17th *arrondissement.*

Gifts

Replicas from museum exhibits and objects by famous manufacturers are sold in four boutiques of the Association Paris-Musées:
Carnavalet
23 rue de Sévigné, 75003. Métro: St-Paul.

Forum des Halles
rue Pierre Lescot. Métro: Les Halles.
Le Louvre
Métro: Palais-Royal.
Galliéra
10 avenue Pierre I de Serbie, 75016. Métro: Iéna.
(See also **Les Bouquinistes**, *p100.)*

Music

Three superstores compete to offer the best prices and a vast choice:
FNAC
Forum des Halles, 1 rue Pierre Lescot. Tel: 01 40 41 40 00. Métro: Les Halles, RER: Châtelet-les-Halles.

FNAC Etoile
26 avenue des Ternes. Tel: 01 44 09 18 00. Métro: Ternes.

Virgin Megastore
52–60 avenue des Champs-Elysées. Tel: 01 49 53 50 00. Métro: Franklin-Roosevelt.

Jewellery

Look for fashion jewellery in **Le Printemps,** the **Galeries Lafayette** *(see p145),* and the **Galerie Vivienne** *(see p97).* The top jewellers – **Boucheron, Cartier, Van Cleef & Arpels** – are in the place Vendôme.

Leather Goods

Rue Tronchet, rue St-Lazare, and adjacent streets (métro St-Lazare), boulevard St-Michel and nearby (métro St-Michel), rue des Archives, Marais (métro Hôtel de Ville).

Luxury Goods

Rue Royale (china, crystal), Champs Elysées (perfumes).

For most people, Paris fashion suggests a dreamworld of elegance, refinement, fantasy, and originality that has helped create the glamorous image of the French capital.

Only a few designers and creators belong to the exclusive club of *haute couture* (literally 'high dressmaking') whose very existence depends on the collections. These are feverishly prepared in great secrecy and revealed during ritual fashion shows in January and June for designer clothes, March and October for *prêt-à-porter* (ready-to-wear). The media plays an essential role in these sophisticated 'performances', in which the top models are the stars. The designers create made-to-measure, very expensive outfits for a mainly foreign clientele. Behind the scenes, a whole army of *petites mains* (seamstresses), embroiderers, milliners, and so on, work endless hours to realise the masterpieces. The creators, on the other hand, concentrate their efforts on *prêt-à-porter*, accessories, and perfumes, initiating new styles and trends that are copied by clothes manufacturers everywhere.

Well apart from the glittering world of designer clothes, the Sentier district (rue Réaumur and side streets, métro Sentier) houses a thousand or so stylists who are in direct contact with retail shops, and who test a limited number of designs. They then mass-produce the most successful ones in the space of a few days. Major projects are under consideration to consolidate the success of the lucrative but vulnerable fashion industry. A *maison de la mode* (headquarters of fashion) has been built under the place du Carrousel at the Louvre, and there are plans for a *cité internationale de la mode* near La Villette. However, above all, several specialised schools ensure that the young designers of tomorrow are being

trained to follow in the footsteps of Cardin, Givenchy, Yves St-Laurent, Christian Dior, Chanel, and a score of household names that, despite repeated offensives from Milan, New York, London, and Tokyo, have maintained Paris as the uncontested world capital of fashion.

Paris chic – enviable, inimitable – embodied by its women, its designers, its models

Entertainment

There are numerous opportunities for entertainment of every kind, whether cultural or not, for the whole family, or for adults only, by day or by night.

IMAX Theatre, La Défense

What's On

The Office du Tourisme et des Congrès de Paris brings out two publications: an annual one called *Saisons de Paris,* which lists the main events (festivals, exhibitions, concerts, etc); and the more detailed monthly, *Paris Sélection,* which has a special section devoted to young people, some useful addresses, and shopping suggestions.

You can also ring **Paris Sélection Loisirs** *(tel: 01 49 52 53 56)* at any time of day or night to get pre-recorded weekly information in English. Furthermore, there are two excellent weekly publications in French (both out on Wednesday), costing only a few Euros; *Pariscope,* which also includes an English section published by *Time Out,* and *L'Officiel des Spectacles.* They include up-to-date admission charges, and a special listing of restaurants open after midnight.

Tickets

Tickets for the theatre, concerts, and other shows can be obtained directly or from the agencies listed below, through whom advance bookings can be made from abroad. This is strongly recommended as performances can be booked up very quickly.

Spectaplus, 252 rue du Faubourg St- Honoré, 75008. *Tel: 01 53 53 58 60; fax: 01 53 53 58 61.* Métro: Charles-de-Gaulle-Etoile.

FNAC Billeterie, all over Paris. *Tel: 08 03 80 88 03.*

Agence Perrosier, 6 place de la Madeleine, 75008. *Tel: 01 42 60 58 31; fax: 01 42 60 14 83.* Métro: Madeleine.

Virgin Megastore, 52–60 Champs Elysées, 75008. *Tel: 08 03 02 30 24.* Métro: Franklin-Roosevelt.

Half-price tickets for performances the same day are available from the following kiosks: 15 place de la Madeleine, 75008 *(tel: 01 47 59 04 04;* open: Tue–Sat 12.30– 8pm, Sun till 4pm; métro: Madeleine), and inside the Châtelet-les-Halles RER station, 75001; (open: Tue–Sat 12.30–8pm).

Cinemas

Cinemas do well in Paris, and film reviews regularly merit extensive coverage in the weekly 'what's on' publications. There is always a good choice of new releases, called *exclusivités,* and of old films, called *reprises,* often shown *en version originale – v o* for short (in the original language) – particularly on the Champs Elysées, in the Latin Quarter, and Odéon district. Large cinemas have several auditoriums, each showing a different film; for instance, the George V at 144 and 146 avenue des Champs Elysées has no fewer than 11 auditoriums, the Gaumont Ambassade at No. 50 has seven, and there are several other multiple cinemas along the 'Champs', as well as three in the Forum des Halles.

Some cinemas go in for festivals devoted to famous directors or actors: for instance, 'Hommage à Frank Capra', 'La Légende Bogart', or 'Viva James Bond!'. Classics are shown in the *cinémathèques* of the Palais de Chaillot and of the Palais de Tokyo (métro Trocadéro), as well as in the Centre Pompidou (métro Rambuteau), while the *vidéothèque* of the Forum des Halles (métro Les Halles) mainly shows documentaries.

In most cinemas prices are reduced on Mondays. On other days children, students, and sometimes senior citizens are entitled to a reduction.

Theatres

The most prestigious of them all, the Comédie Française, also called Le Théâtre Français or simply Le Français (2 rue de Richelieu, 75001, *tel: 01 44 58 15 15*; métro Palais-Royal. *Also see p94*), traditionally puts on the great French classical comedies and tragedies by Molière, Racine, and other masters. Its repertoire also includes selected 20th-century French and foreign plays. The acting is usually superb. The following theatres put on good productions of modern French and foreign plays. Booking starts two weeks in advance.

L'Atelier
Place Charles-Dullin, 75018.
Tel: 01 46 06 49 24. Métro: Anvers.

Cartoucherie (Théâtre du Soleil)
Route du Champ-des-Manoeuvres, 75012.

Tel: 01 43 74 24 08.
Métro: Château de Vincennes,
then shuttle service.

Espace Critic
(Espace Cardin), 1 avenue Gabriel, 75008.
Tel: 01 42 66 17 30. Métro: Concorde.

Espace Marais
22 rue Beautreillis, 75004.
Tel: 01 48 04 91 55. Métro: St-Paul.

Hébertot
78 bis boulevard des Batignolles, 75017.
Tel: 01 43 87 23 23.
Métro: Villiers or Rome.

Huchette
Eugène Ionesco plays.
23 rue de la Huchette, 75005.
Tel: 01 43 26 38 99. Métro: St-Michel.

Lucernaire Centre National d'Art et d'Essai
53 rue Notre-Dame-des-Champs, 75006.
Tel: 01 45 44 57 34. Métro: Vavin.

Odéon Théâtre de l'Europe
Place Paul Claudel, 75006.
Tel: 01 44 41 36 38. Métro: Odéon.

Théâtre National de Chaillot
1 place du Trocadéro, 75016.
Tel: 01 53 65 31 00. Métro: Trocadéro.

Paris offers many choices to cinema-goers

Café Life

The French café is an institution; it is not a bar, that is not subtle enough, it is not a pub, that is not Latin enough, it is not a wine bar either, although it does sell wine. In a word, the French café is unique. Most visitors to France know that, and their faces light up at the thought of indulging an hour or two sitting on the crowded terrace of a café watching the world go by.

Cafés are busy all day. They open early in the morning in time to serve the traditional *grand crème* (large cup of white coffee) with croissants to people on their way to work. Throughout the day they serve wine by the glass, beer – *un demi* (originally ½ litre, just over a pint), or *une pression* (a glass of draught beer) – or *un pastis*, a strong aniseed

drink diluted with water, and, of course, the tiny *espresso*, a cup of strong black coffee that seems to keep French people

going. Drinks are cheaper *au bar* (standing at the bar) than *en salle* (sitting at one of the typical round tables). You can always spot the *garçon* (waiter) with his black trousers, white shirt and black waistcoat, as he makes his way through the crowd with great agility.

The local cafés where 'regulars' have their drink at 11am, working people eat a quick snack at lunchtime, and local residents meet in the evening to catch up on the news, play an important role in the city's social life. They have nothing in common with the elegant establishments of the place de l'Opéra, full of wealthy tourists and retired Parisians, or even with the Left Bank cafés where a fashionable élite goes to be seen!

Variety in an unpressured atmosphere: a leisurely *petit déjeuner*, a mid-morning pick-me-up, a range of hot options, an observation post on society

Music

As soon as the season ends in June, festivals take over, so that there is always a wide choice of concerts.

Classical Concerts

Paris has many orchestras, from the chamber ensemble to the symphony orchestra. The most prestigious are the Orchestre National de France, the Orchestre Philharmonique de Radio France, the Orchestre de Paris, and the Ensemble Intercontemporain. The main venues vary in size from the small **Salle Gaveau** to the vast **Théâtre des Champs Elysées** and the **Salle Pleyel.** There are lunchtime or early evening concerts in many churches throughout the capital, concerts in parks and gardens from May to September, and a recently launched operation, *Monuments en Musique,* which provides short musical programmes at regular intervals in selected monuments.

Opera and Ballet

Most major operas are now staged at the **Opéra Bastille,** but the **Opéra Garnier** seems to be getting its share again, when technical conditions permit. The rest of the time it is the exclusive home of ballet. The Orchestre de l'Opéra de Paris, which is shared between the two houses, is one of the top orchestras in the country.

Jazz, Rock, and Pop Music

Concerts are usually held in large venues such as the new **Zénith** at La Villette *(see p117)*, the **Palais Omnisports Paris Bercy** (boulevard de Bercy, 75012; métro Bercy), and the **Palais des** Congrès (Porte Maillot, 75017; métro Porte-Maillot). The old **Olympia** music hall (boulevard des Capucines, 75009; métro Opéra) is the traditional venue for variety shows, and all aspiring artists hope to top the bill there.

Nightlife

Like most capital cities, Paris has a large number of bars, discos, nightclubs, and sex shows (the latter mainly in the sleazy Pigalle area), but its cabaret shows are still considered the most typically French form of night entertainment.

Cabarets

These became famous at the turn of the century, partly for their lavish, colourful productions and partly because they shocked the predominantly bourgeois society. Today they no longer shock, but the productions are just as lavish.

Moulin Rouge

Probably the most famous, with its 'girls' dancing the French cancan.
82 boulevard de Clichy, 75018.
Tel: 01 53 09 82 82.

Folies Bergère
32 rue Richer, 75009. Tel: 01 44 79 98 98.

Lido

Very sophisticated light effects.
116 bis avenue des Champs Elysées, 75008. Tel: 01 40 76 56 10.

Crazy Horse Saloon

Reputed to be the most 'with it' of all.
12 avenue George V, 75008.
Tel: 01 47 23 57 35.

Jazz Clubs

Very popular, also very crowded; arrive early but don't expect things to get going before 11pm.

Au Duc des Lombards
Small, cozy club.
42 rue des Lombards, 75001. Tel: 01 42 33 22 88. Métro: Chalet-les-Halles.

Bilboquet
Jazz club in *belle-époque* setting.
13 rue St-Benoit, 75006. Tel: 01 45 48 81 84. Métro: St-Germain-des-Prés.

Caveau de la Huchette
Authentic jazz cellars with dancing (rock 'n' roll) to live orchestra.
5 rue de la Huchette, 75005. Tel: 01 43 26 65 05. Métro: St-Michel.

La Villa
Chic and cosy jazz club in small St-Germain-des-Prés hotel.
29 rue Jacob, 75006. Tel: 01 43 26 60 00. Métro: St-Germain-des-Prés.

New Morning
Jazz and world music venue featuring internationally acclaimed musicians.
7/9 rue des Petites-Ecuries, 75010. Tel: 01 45 23 51 41. Métro: Château-d'eau.

Petit Journal Montparnasse
Blues, African, and traditional jazz.
13 rue du Commandant, Mouchotte, 75014. Tel: 01 43 21 56 70. Métro: Gaîté.

Nightclubs
These liven up from midnight onwards.

Les Bains
Nightclub in old public baths.
7 rue du Bourg-l'Abbé, 75003. Tel: 01 48 87 01 80. Métro: Etienne Marcel.

Niel's
Haunt of press and showbiz people.
27 avenue des Ternes, 75017. Tel: 01 47 66 45 00. Métro: Ternes.

La Locomotive
Trendy nightclub near Montmartre.
90 boulevard de Clichy. Tel: 08 36 69 69 28.

La Scala
Special effects with laser lights.
188 bis rue de Rivoli, 75001. Tel: 01 42 61 64 00.

The famous Moulin Rouge

Children

Paris and the Ile-de-France offer children of all ages a choice of entertaining activities, whatever the weather.

Monuments

A climb up the Eiffel Tower will thrill youngsters of all ages, while older ones will enjoy the Conciergerie and its gruesome stories, the Château de Vincennes, and Versailles.

Museums

The Musée Grévin in the boulevard Montmartre, with its wax figures of famous historical and contemporary characters, is both entertaining and educational *(see p86)*.

Quite a few museums organise special activities for children of different age groups; the Cité des Sciences et de l'Industrie at la Villette *(see pp116–17)* offers an introduction to science and technology called **l'Inventorium** with workshops for 3- to 6- and 6- to 12-year-olds; robots, computers, and audio-visual games encourage children to participate, and there are special shows at the planetarium.

Jardin des Tuileries, one of Paris's many monuments and parks to be enjoyed by all ages

The Centre Georges Pompidou *(see pp36–7)* aims to help children discover art through workshops based on current exhibitions.

On Wednesday afternoons, at the **Musée d'Orsay** *(see pp82–3)*, there are guided visits of the collections based on a theme, as well as workshops for 5- to 10-year olds.

The **Palais de la Découverte** *(see p26)* has chemistry and astronomy workshops for teenagers.

In the **Musée des Arts d'Afrique et d'Océanie** *(see p123)*, there is a huge tropical aquarium with turtles, crocodiles, and sharks, which never fails to impress children.

The World of the Sea
Tropical Aquarium
Musée des Arts d'Afrique et d'Océanie, 293 avenue Daumesnil, 75012. Tel: 01 43 46 51 61. Open: Mon & Wed–Fri 10am–noon & 1.30–5.30pm, Sat & Sun 10am–6pm. Closed: Tue. Admission charge. Métro: Porte Doué.
L'Argonaute
A real submarine at the
Cité de Sciences et de l'Industrie at La Villette, 211 avenue Jean-Jaurès, 75019. Tel: 01 40 05 83 28. Open: Tue–Sun 10am–6pm. Closed: Mon. Admission charge. Métro: Porte de Pantin.
Centre de la Mer et des Eaux
At this marine and freshwater centre, simple phenomena are explained

through observation, games, and audio-visual presentations.

195 rue St-Jacques, 75005. Tel: 01 44 32 10 70. Open Tue–Fri 10am–12.30pm & 1.15–5.30pm, Sat & Sun 10am–5.30pm. Closed: Mon. Admission charge. Métro: Luxembourg.

Parks and Gardens
Jardin d'Acclimatation
In the Bois de Boulogne this is an amusement park for children of all ages. A little train runs a shuttle service between the Porte Maillot and the park on Wednesday, Saturday, and Sunday afternoons, and during school holidays.
Bois de Boulogne, 75016. Tel: 01 40 67 90 82. Open: 10am–6pm. Admission charge. Métro: Porte Maillot (little train) or Sablons.

The Jardin des Enfants
An adventure playground for 7- to 11-year olds at La Halle.
105 rue Rambuteau, 75003. Tel: 01 45 08 07 18. Métro: Les Halles.

While most parks in the capital have a children's play area, three are better equipped. The **Parc des Buttes-Chaumont** *(see p140)* has lots of space and plenty of attractions, including rock-climbing for older children. The **Parc Gëorges Brassens** *(see p140)* has wooden huts in a miniature forest setting with rocks to match, as well as the usual attractions. **The Parc Floral de Paris** in the Bois de Vincennes *(see p123)* aims to initiate children in the pleasures of a nature trail.

Zoos
There is a small zoo in the **Jardin des**

The perfect match: kids and open space

Plantes *(see p140)* and another in the **Bois de Vincennes** *(see p123)*.

Fun with Water
Aquaboulevard
An aquatic adventure playground. It offers such attractions as giant slides and a bubble pool.
4–6 rue Louis-Armand, 75015. Tel: 01 40 60 10 10. Open: 9am–midnight. Admission charge. Métro: Balard.

In fine weather, children will enjoy a boat trip on the **Lac Inférieur** in the Bois de Boulogne or on the **Lac Daumesnil** in the Bois de Vincennes, and also a trip on the Seine in one of the **Bateaux Mouches** boats *(see p186)*.

Shows
There are *Guignol* (Punch and Judy) shows in most public parks and gardens. Paris also has a number of circuses which move about according to the season. Ring the following for the latest information on performances:
Cirque Bouglione, *tel: 01 47 00 12 25.*
Cirque Bormann, *tel: 01 45 00 23 01.*
Cirque Gruss, *tel: 01 40 36 08 00.*

Sport and Leisure

Regular television coverage of sports events has contributed to a change of attitude towards sport in France, and particularly in Paris. Sport has entered every home, and the number of spectators has reached phenomenal proportions. As a result, more money has been invested in making sport accessible to a wider public. Stadiums and large indoor venues have been modernised, and facilities for individual sports have improved.

The Tour de France goes past the Eiffel Tower

Sports Centres and Stadiums

More than 500 national and international sports events take place every year in the city's main venues.

Palais Omnisports de Paris-Bercy Built in 1984, this is a huge, multi-purpose centre where 150 different events take place annually. The seating capacity can be adapted to each event, with a maximum of 17,000. There is also an ice-skating rink, numerous dressing rooms, and a medical centre. It is also frequently used for rock concerts (8 boulevard de Bercy, 75012; *tel: 01 40 02 60 60/08 03 03 00 31;* métro: Bercy).

With a capacity of 50,000 spectators, the **Parc des Princes**, situated in an affluent residential district just south of the Bois de Boulogne, is the main venue for football and rugby matches (24 rue du Commandant-Guilbaud, 75016; *tel: 01 42 88 02 76;* métro: Exelmans or Porte de St-Cloud).

Quite close is the famous **Stade Roland-Garros**, a tennis complex with 16 courts, including a centre court with room for 16,500 spectators (2 avenue Gordon-Bennett, 75016; *tel: 01 47 43*

48 00; métro: Porte d'Auteuil). Next to it, on the edge of the Bois de Boulogne, are two of the capital's three racecourses: the **Hippodrome d'Auteuil** (place de la Porte d'Auteuil; *tel: 01 40 71 47 47;* métro: Porte d'Auteuil), famous for steeplechasing, and the **Hippodrome de Longchamp** (boulevard Anatole-France; *tel: 01 44 30 75 00;* métro: Porte d'Auteuil, then shuttle bus). The third racecourse is the **Hippodrome de Vincennes** on the other side of town (2 route de la Ferme, 75012; *tel: 01 49 77 17 17;* RER Joinville-le-Pont).

Still in the 16th *arrondissement,* the **Stade Pierre de Coubertin** stages events such as judo and fencing competitions, gymnastics and dance displays, boxing and basketball matches (82 avenue Georges-Lafont, 75016; *tel: 01 45 27 79 12;* métro: Porte de St-Cloud).

The Stade Georges Carpentier holds indoor sports competitions such as martial arts, volleyball, badminton, and table tennis (81 boulevard Masséna, 75013; *tel: 01 42 16 66 00;* métro: Porte d'Ivry or Porte de Choisy).

The vast new **Stade Charléty**, with a capacity of 20,000 spectators, hosts both outdoor and indoor sports, from football to athletics, and tennis (1 avenue de la porte de Gentilly, 75013; *tel: 01 44 16 60 60;* métro: Cité Universitaire).

Built for the 1924 Olympic Games, the **Georges Vallerey swimming pool** saw Johnny Weissmüller of Tarzan fame beat the world 400m freestyle record. Entirely modernised in 1989, it can now hold water polo events, as well as international swimming competitions (148 avenue Gambetta, 75020; *tel: 01 40 31 15 20;* métro: Porte des Lilas).

SPECTATOR SPORTS
Cycling
The colourful and often dramatic finish of the Tour de France is staged along the Champs Elysées.

Football
The Coupe de France is held in the Parc des Princes in April or May.

Racing
There are two racecourses on the south side of the Bois de Boulogne. Auteuil specialises in steeple chasing and is famous for its difficult jumps. Flat racing takes place at Longchamp. Prestigious races such as the Prix du Président de la République on Palm Sunday, or the Grand Prix de l'Arc de Triomphe on the first Sunday in October, draw fashionable crowds who come more to be seen than to watch the racing. The Vincennes racecourse, situated on the other side of town, is popular for trotting events.

Rugby
The Tournoi des Six Nations, involving England, Scotland, Wales, Ireland, France, and Italy, is held at the Parc des Princes.

Running
The famous Marathon de Paris takes place in the capital in March or April.

Tennis
The Championnats Internationaux de France (French Open) take place at the Stade Roland-Garros in late May and early June. The Open de la Ville de Paris is held in the Palais Omnisports de Paris-Bercy in late October.

A keenly watched tennis match in progress

PARTICIPATORY SPORTS

There are more than 250 locations all over Paris where amateurs and professionals can practise the sport of their choice. Municipal equipment is available to everyone for a very modest fee, and visitors may join certain private clubs on a temporary basis.

To get the best information on what is available in your area, contact the Office Municipal des Sports in the *mairie d'arrondissement* (district town hall). You can also obtain from the *mairie* a booklet entitled *Centre d'Animation Magazine*, published twice yearly, which contains a list of all sports centres, with addresses and programmes. *Sport à la carte* has been specially devised to provide individual programmes in municipal centres at fixed hours.

Bowling

This has been popular with young people for some time, more as a leisure activity than a sport.

Bowling Champerret
place Porte Champerret, 75017. Tel: 01 43 80 24 64. Open: daily 10am–2am. Bar. Métro: Porte de Champerret.

Bowling Foch
8 avenue Foch, 75016. Tel: 01 45 00 00 13. Open: daily 11am–2am. Bar. Métro: Etoile.

Bowling Montparnasse
27 rue Commandant-Mouchotte, 75014. Tel: 01 43 21 61 32. Open: daily 10am–2am (4am on Fri & Sat). Bar-restaurant. Métro: Montparnasse.

Climbing

Three new structures have been installed in the city to accommodate the growing number of enthusiasts; the most impressive is located at the **Stade des Poissonniers**
2 rue Jean-Cocteau, 75018. Tel: 01 42 51 24 68. Open: Wed 2.30–5pm. Maximum height: 21m. Métro: Porte de Clignancourt.

For other possibilities and information contact the Fédération Française de la Montagne et de l'Escalade (20 bis rue de la Boétie, 75008, *tel: 01 40 18 75 50).*

Cycling

Nearly 400 clubs in the Paris region organise tours in Ile-de-France. For information contact:
Fédération Française de Cyclisme
5 rue de Rome, 75008. Tel: 01 49 35 69 00.

Golf

Several clubs and centres offer golfers the possibility of practising putting, and even their drive, with the help of simulators. However, the real thing takes place out of town. For detailed information contact:
Fédération Française de Golf
68 Anatole France, Levallois Perret, 92300. Tel: 01 41 49 77 00.

Gymnastics and Fitness

Many clubs specialise in keep-fit classes, aerobics, body-building, swimming, etc. Equipped with saunas and Jacuzzis, they are usually restricted 'members only' clubs. One of the most sophisticated is:
Espace Vit'Halles
48 rue Rambuteau, 75003. Tel: 01 42 77 21 71. Métro: Rambuteau, Les Halles.

Swimming

There are many municipal swimming pools in Paris as well as a number of private ones. The following is a selection of the most attractive:

Piscine Deligny
A floating pool.
Along the quai Anatole-France, 75007.
Tel: 01 45 55 89 19. Métro: Solférino.

Piscine Jean Taris
Lovely Japanese garden setting.
16 rue Thouin, 75005. Tel: 01 43 25 54 03.
Métro: Cardinal-Lemoine.

Piscine des Halles
An Olympic-size pool with a view of the tropical glasshouse.
Forum des Halles. Tel: 01 42 36 98 44.
Métro: Les Halles.

Tennis and Squash

There are 150 municipal tennis courts open until 10pm, available by the hour at very reasonable fees. For detailed information, contact the local *mairie* (town hall) or Allo Sports *(see p188)*. In addition, there are several private clubs:

Squash Montmartre
Four courts, clubhouse, restaurant.
14 rue Achille Martinet, 75018.
Tel: 01 42 55 38 30. Métro: Lamarck.

Squash-Golf Rennes Raspail
Seven courts and golf practice.
149 rue de Rennes, 75006.
Tel: 01 44 39 03 30. Métro: Rennes.

Tennis de Longchamp
20 courts.
19 boulevard Anatole-France, 92 Boulogne. Tel: 01 46 03 84 49.
Métro: Porte d'Auteuil.

Watersports

Waterskiing and canoeing are now possible at the new **Bassin de la Villette** *(5 bis quai de la Loire, 75019; métro: Jaurès or Stalingrad).*

Leisure Parks Outside Paris

Activities include swimming, sailing, windsurfing, riding, and tennis.

Parc de Loisirs Torcy Marne-la-Vallée, route de Lagny
77 Torcy. 25km east of Paris.
Tel: 01 64 80 58 75. Open: 9am– 6pm.
RER: Torcy-Marne-la-Vallée.

Le Val de Seine
78480 Verneuil-sur-Seine. 30km (18 miles) west of Paris. Tel: 01 39 71 07 06.
Open: 9am–noon, 2–6pm.

Cycling in the Bois de Boulogne

Food and Drink

Food is an important ingredient of the French way of life and some of the rituals that accompany its preparation and consumption are still performed by a majority of French people, even in Paris where the pressures of modern city life seem to go against the more traditional principles of gastronomy.

Takeaway food in a class by itself

Eating Habits

The French are particular about 'fresh' food: bread, meat, and vegetables are usually bought daily. A lot of people shop after working hours, which explains why food shops and markets stay open late. The time spent on cooking varies, but has been considerably shortened for working people, thanks to the mouth-watering, freshly prepared dishes sold in the numerous *charcuteries*.

Although two main meals a day is usual, around midday and 8pm, in Paris lunch tends to be reduced to a quick light meal, the emphasis being on the evening meal served with wine. A family meal generally comprises one type of wine, usually red, though special meals include at least two different wines, carefully chosen to go with each dish. Some people drink beer with their meals, and nearly everyone drinks mineral water and fruit juice some time during the day. Breakfast is not very copious: freshly bought bread with butter and jam, marmalade or honey, and/or a croissant. *Boulangeries* open early so people can drop in for fresh supplies before going to work. *Café au lait*, or *café crème* (white coffee) as it is

called in cafés, is still the popular breakfast drink, but more people are drinking black coffee these days, and tea is gaining in popularity.

Shopping for Food

Food shops have a place of honour in the best districts, and some of them have elaborate, imaginative displays worthy of shops selling luxury goods – that is exactly what they are doing!

Shopping Streets and Markets

Each district has an open-air market as well as one or two streets, often pedestrianised during part of the day, where food shops are concentrated and stalls are set up on the pavement to promote certain kinds of produce. Prices can vary considerably; the accent is on friendliness, and customers are invited to select what they want. Basic shops always include one or two *boucheries* (butchers), *boulangeries-pâtisseries* (bakers), *crémeries-fromageries* (dairies), *charcuteries* (delicatessens), and *poissonneries* (fishmongers).

The following streets are renowned for good quality and good value:
Near Les Halles: the rue Montorgueil, which still keeps alive the atmosphere of

the old central food market *(see p54)*, and the rue Rambuteau.

In the 17th arrondissement: the rue Poncelet near the place des Ternes, where there is one of the best coffee shops in Paris, the Brûlerie des Ternes at No. 10, and the rue de Lévis near the Parc Monceau.

On the Left Bank: the rue Mouffetard, the rue de Buci and the rue de Seine, probably the most picturesque in Paris.

Specialised Shops

Cheese can be bought in supermarkets, *épiceries* (grocers), and from market stalls, but connoisseurs prefer to select from one of the 300 different cheeses made in France at a reputed *fromager* who can recommend the best *brebis* (ewes' milk cheese) or the tastiest *chevrotin* (goats' milk cheese from Savoie), or a superb *Pont-l'Evêque* (a famous cows' milk cheese from Normandy).

Androuët (41 rue d'Amsterdam, 75008; métro: Liège) is something of a legend, with over 200 varieties kept at the right temperature in the cellars. **Lionel Poilâne** (8 rue du Cherche-Midi, 75006; métro: Sèvres-Babylone), adept at authenticity, is undoubtedly the most famous baker in Paris, while the *pâtisserie* **Lenôtre** (48 avenue Victor-Hugo, 75016; métro: Victor-Hugo), is unequalled for imagination and refinement. **Berthillon** (31 rue St-Louis-en-l'Ile, 75004; métro: Pont-Marie) is the best place for ice cream, and has some unusual flavours.

The Madeleine area (métro: Madeleine) has several luxury food shops, including the famous **Fauchon** (26 place de la Madeleine), an *épicerie fine* (luxury grocer), and delicatessen whose displays are real works of art, and the more modest **Hédiard** at No. 21. Next door at No. 19 is the **Maison de la Truffe,** where you can buy fresh truffles as well as delicious *charcuterie*. Nearby, in the rue Vignon, is the **Maison du Miel** at No. 24, where you can taste and buy all kinds of rare honey.

Goats' milk cheese in its many forms

Cuisine

It is a well-known, although controversial fact that 'Paris is not France'; the French themselves acknowledge it, especially if they are not Parisians. Yet, paradoxically, although there is no Parisian cuisine as such, Paris has become a melting pot of the best culinary traditions, and the undisputed capital of French gastronomy.

Variety is the first and foremost characteristic of French cuisine. The ingredients used in cooking have regional origins; cream, butter, and

cheese are widely used in northern areas where milk products are plentiful, while olive oil and garlic are typical of Mediterranean areas; red wine makes casseroles rich and tasty in the Bourgogne district.

The universal fame of traditional French cuisine rests on the variety of its regional dishes.

Among starters, you may find *hors-d'oeuvre variés* (raw vegetables seasoned with oil and vinegar, served with assorted *charcuterie*), *quiche lorraine* (savoury flan with pieces of

bacon), *moules marinière* (mussels simmered in white wine with shallots), or the delicious *soupe à l'onion gratinée* (onion soup with melted cheese).

Main dishes usually include several of the following: *entrecôte bordelaise* (juicy steak with a rich wine sauce), *boeuf bourguignon* (casseroled beef with onions and mushrooms, in a red Burgundy wine), *blanquette de veau* (stewed veal with cream and mushrooms), and *choucroute garnie* (sauerkraut cooked in dry white wine, with pork and sausages). *Gratin dauphinois* (sliced potatoes baked with cream and grated cheese) is ideal with tasty grills.

To finish a good meal, there is nothing more refreshing than a home-baked *crème caramel* (egg custard coated with caramel), or a cool *baba-au-rhum* (light sponge cake with rum syrup).

However, French cuisine does not rely for its success on tradition alone, for it is constantly being reinvented and perfected by ambitious young chefs whose imagination has no bounds.

Variety and quality are essential components of traditional French cuisine

Casual al fresco dining in Montmartre

Eating Out

The choice is vast and there are places to suit every occasion, from the local, inexpensive *bistro* to the exclusive temple of gastronomy, from fast-food bars and quaint tearooms to regional and exotic ethnic restaurants.

Each type of establishment has its own personality and represents a different aspect of Parisian life. Crowded at lunchtime, cafés are ideal for a quick meal, with a restricted menu usually consisting of *steak/frites* (steak and chips), mixed salads, and a selection of sandwiches made with crisp *baguettes* (French bread). Slightly more expensive, *brasseries* offer a choice of traditional dishes that include an Alsatian *choucroute garnie* (sauerkraut with assorted sausages) served with beer or wine. Top *brasseries* have an attractive display of fresh seafood just outside

their premises with an attendant serving oysters and other pricey delicacies to passers-by and preparing orders for customers inside. There are several such establishments on the place de Clichy, not far from the Moulin Rouge.

Wine bars are not steeped in tradition like cafés and *brasseries*, but they seem to fit in well with the Parisians' changing lifestyle, and are becoming increasingly popular as a lunchtime venue. They serve an assortment of cold platters and cheese with selected wines by the glass, thus enabling the real amateur to taste and enjoy excellent wine without having to buy a full bottle. **L'Ecluse,** 15 quai des Grands-Augustins, 75006; métro: St-Michel, is one of the most famous, and a good place to sample for atmosphere.

Little known or talked about are the discreet but charming *salons de thé* (tearooms), often tucked away in picturesque arcades. They offer the luxury of a relaxed atmosphere in refined surroundings, and serve good-quality snacks and pastries with a choice of fine teas or coffee. Two of the best are: **Angélina,** 226 rue de Rivoli, near the Jardin des Tuileries, and **La Cour de Rohan,** Cour du Commerce St-André, off the rue St-André-des-Arts, near the place St-Michel.

The name restaurant applies to a wide range of establishments, from the unassuming, friendly, local place with white lace curtains at the windows and rickety tables outside in summertime, to the select, fashionable, outrageously expensive, or just exquisitely refined rendezvous for gourmets. The variety stems from the type of cuisine served, whether French or ethnic. Typical cuisines from the regions of France are well represented by authentic chefs who have come to the capital to make a name for themselves. In some cases they are concentrated in a specific area. For instance, exponents of Breton cuisine are grouped in the vicinity of the Gare Montparnasse, while specialities from the Auvergne are to be found in the Bastille area.

The number of ethnic restaurants has increased lately and they, too, tend to congregate in specific areas, sometimes taking over a whole street, like the rue de la Huchette, near the place St-Michel, which is lined with cheap Greek and North African restaurants. The rue des Rosiers and adjacent streets in the Marais are well known for their Jewish and East European restaurants. The 13th *arrondissement*, near the Porte d'Ivry, where Asian restaurants are plentiful, has been christened 'Chinatown'. By contrast, you hardly notice the less conspicuous presence of several Japanese restaurants in the Opéra district.

Choosing a Restaurant

It is difficult to generalise about value for money as quality and prices vary a lot. On the whole, however, one may say that, in the lower price range, value for money – both in quantity and quality – is better in Paris than in most Western capitals. This tends to be less true in the upper price range, but Paris still retains a slight advantage as far as service, attention to detail, and imagination are concerned.

The price range given in the listings below refers to an average meal per person, not including drinks. There are four categories:

★	Less than €30.5
★★	€30.5–45.7
★★★	€45.7–76.2
★★★	Over €76.2

Wine with your meal can cost from around 9 Euros a bottle to a hundred Euros for a château wine.

Most restaurants offer a fixed-price menu (some at lunchtime only) which is better value for money than *à la carte* (chosen from the larger selection of dishes). In any case, 15 per cent service charge is usually included in the price.

Rabbit, anyone? Lapin Agile, Montmartre

The restaurants selected are located in nine areas covered most extensively in this book.

Where to Eat
MARAIS, ILE ST-LOUIS
L'Ambroisie ★★★★
Superb cuisine and refined decor in a restored jeweller's shop. Reservations essential; book at least one month ahead.
9 place des Vosges, 75004.
Tel: 01 42 78 51 45.
Métro: Bastille.
Bouchon du Marais ★
Specialities are fondue and cheese dishes.
1 rue François Miron, 75004. Tel: 01 48 87 44 13.
Métro: St-Paul, Hôtel de Ville.
Nos Ancêtres les Gaulois ★
Four courses for a fixed price and unlimited wine in a convivial pseudo-medieval setting.
39 rue St-Louis-en-l'Ile, 75004. Tel: 01 46 33 66 07.
Métro: Pont-Marie.

LES HALLES
Au Pied de Cochon ★
An old classic from market days at Les Halles. Serves traditional onion soup. Good place for pigs' trotters.
6 rue Coquillière, 75001.
Tel: 01 42 36 11 75.
Métro: Les Halles.
Benoît ★★
The typical old-fashioned bistro atmosphere.
20 rue St-Martin, 75004.
Tel: 01 42 72 25 76.
Métro: Châtelet.
Gérard Besson ★★★
Authentic gourmet cuisine; elegant, comfortable decor.
5 rue Coq-Héron, 75001.
Tel: 01 42 33 14 74.
Métro: Louvre.

PALAIS-ROYAL, OPERA, CONCORDE
Le Grand Café Capucines ★★
One of the top brasseries serving excellent seafood.
4 boulevard des Capucines, 75009. Tel: 01 43 12 19 00.
Métro: Opéra.
Lucas-Carton ★★★★
Supervised by one of Paris's top chefs. Beautiful *belle-époque* architecture. Try the roast duck with honey and spices.
9 place de la Madeleine, 75008. Tel: 01 42 65 22 90.
Métro: Madeleine.
Maxim's ★★★★
Probably the most prestigious restaurant in Paris; reservations essential.
3 rue Royale, 75008.
Tel: 01 42 65 27 94.
Métro: Concorde.

Waiting to serve you with French flair

ETOILE, CHAMPS ELYSEES
Le Fouquet's ★★★
Experience the Parisian scene at this rendezvous of film stars and celebrities.
99 avenue des Champs-Elysées, 75008.
Tel: 01 47 23 50 00.
Métro: George V.
La Fermette Marbeuf ★★
Fashionable but unpretentious restaurant, excellent low-priced menu in the evening.
5 rue Marbeuf, 75008.
Tel: 01 53 23 08 00.
Métro: Alma-Marceau.
Taillevent ★★★★
19th-century mansion, serving high-class cuisine. Book months ahead.
15 rue Lamennais, 75008.
Tel: 01 44 95 15 01.
Métro: George V.

TROCADERO, PASSY
La Butte Chaillot ★★
Refined cuisine; striking contemporary setting.
110 bis avenue Kléber, 75016. Tel: 01 47 27 88 88.
Métro: Trocadéro.

Alain Ducasse au Plaza Athénée ★★★★
Futuristic design. Inspired cuisine by a great chef.
25 avenue Montaigne, 75008. Tel: 01 53 67 65 00. Métro: Trocadéro.

L'Astrance ★★
A first-rate bistro with contemporary decor.
4 rue Beethoven, 75006. Tel: 01 40 50 84 40. Métro: Plassy.

Le Petit Rétro ★
Suberb traditional cuisine served in a listed monument with 1910s decor.
5 rue Mesnil, 75016. Tel: 01 44 05 06 05. Métro: Victor.

MONTMARTRE

L'Etrier ★★
Refined, traditional French cuisine; good value; book a table.
154 rue Lamarc, 75018. Tel: 01 42 29 14 01. Métro: Guy Môquet.

Le Moulin a Vins ★
Lively and rustic with succulent charcuterie.
6 rue Burg, 75008. Tel: 01 42 52 81 27. Métro: Abbesses.

Le Restaurant ★
In a quiet street of old Montmartre.
32 rue Véron, 75018. Tel: 01 42 23 06 22. Métro: Abbesses.

LATIN QUARTER

L'Atelier de Maître Albert ★★
Fixed-price includes half a bottle of wine.
1 rue Maître-Albert, 75005. Tel: 01 46 33 13 78. Métro: Maubert-Mutualité.

La Tour d'Argent ★★★★
Expensive, excellent food.
15 quai de la Tournelle, 75005. Tel: 01 43 54 23 31. Métro: Maubert-Mutualité.

Le Grenier Notre-Dame ★
Vegetarian restaurant close to Notre-Dame.
18 rue de la Bûcherie, 75005. Tel: 01 43 29 98 29. Métro: Maubert-Mutualité.

ST-GERMAIN-DES-PRÉS

Aux Charpentiers ★
Publishers' haunt.
10 rue Mabillon, 75006. Tel: 01 43 26 30 05. Métro: Mabillon.

Les Bookinistes ★★★
Fashionable restaurant along the embankment.
53 quai des Grands-Augustins, 75006. Tel: 01 43 25 45 94. Métro: St-Michel.

Jacques Cagna ★★★
Magnificent 17th-century house and excellent traditional cuisine.
14 rue des Grands-Augustins, 75006. Tel: 01 43 26 49 39. Métro: St-Michel.

Le Petit Saint Benoit ★
Charming restaurant, simple, unpretentious home cooking.
4 rue Saint Benoit, 75006. Tel: 01 42 60 27 92. Métro: St-Germain-des-Prés.

Le Petit Zinc ★★
Typical Left Bank bistro serving excellent seafood.
11 rue Benoît, 75006. Tel: 01 42 86 61 00. Métro: St-Germain-des-Prés.

Polidor ★
Authentic bistro with convivial atmosphere. Open till late.
41 rue Monsieur-le-Prince, 75006. Tel: 01 43 26 95 34. Métro: Luxembourg.

INVALIDES, FAUBOURG ST-GERMAIN

La Petite Chaise ★
Excellent value.
36 rue de Grenelle, 75007. Tel: 01 42 22 13 35. Métro: Sèvres-Babylone.

Le Divellec ★★★★
A top seafood restaurant.
107 rue de l'Université, 75007. Tel: 01 45 51 91 96. Métro: Invalides.

Vin sur Vin ★★
Close to the Eiffel Tower, copious savoury dishes.
20 rue de Monttessuy, 75007. Tel: 01 47 05 14 20. Métro: Pont de l'Alma.

Wine is the French national drink, its infinite variety matching that of French cuisine. Vines have been grown in France since Roman times, and ancestral traditions are still observed in many regions. Wine-making methods are strictly controlled, and a grading system is applied accordingly.

Vin de table is a cheap, ordinary wine. It is drunk 'young' (within a year). Next comes the *Vin délimité de qualité supérieure* (VDQS), a higher-grade wine produced in areas where quality is constant. *Appellation d'Origine Contrôlée* (AOC) denotes a wine characteristic of a specific district, or *cru*, such as Médoc in the Bordeaux region.

This information and more is on the labels, and it is well worth studying them carefully when selecting a good red or white château wine. Look for the year, as quality varies from year to year, and for the words *mis en bouteilles au château* (bottled at the château); but bear in mind that there are many château wines and the best of them have been graded as *cru bourgeois* and *grand cru* or *1er cru, 2ème cru*, and so on.

The two main wine-producing regions are the Bordeaux region in the southwest with famous wines like Médoc, Graves, St-Emilion, or Pomerol, and Bourgogne in the east, with inspiring names such as Nuits-St-Georges, Chambertin, Pommard, and Pouilly-Fuissé.

Other regions also produce some great wines; for instance, Châteauneuf-du-Pape, which comes from the Rhône

Valley, and Riesling from the Alsace.
Champagne, named after the region in
northeastern France, is in a class of its
own. The lengthy production process
was perfected in the 17th century by
Dom Pérignon, a monk who came from
the abbaye d'Hautvillers.

Wine-bottle shapes vary from one
region to another, providing an
immediate clue to their origins. Thus,
the elegant, slim bottle from the
southwest contrasts with the stockier
type used in Bourgogne and
Champagne, or the tall fluted ones
typical of Alsace.

Whatever your taste, your budget, or the
occasion, there's a bottle of wine to suit it

Hotels and Accommodation

Old and new, traditional and modern, Parisian hotels vary considerably in size and the degree of comfort they offer. During the last few years, many have been renovated, modernised, and refurbished, with the emphasis on proper separate bathroom facilities instead of the usual washbasin and bidet, even in the lowest grade. Only the more expensive hotels have restaurants.

The highly fashionable Ritz hotel, Paris

Grading

The system used is the same as in other regions of France. Hotels are graded by the Direction de l'Industrie Touristique, according to the degree of comfort and quality of services. Present standards were fixed by decree in 1986, and regular checks are carried out by the Préfecture. There are five grades, which can be described as follows:

HT, HRT, or 1-star applies to modest hotels with basic comforts, but bear in mind that standards have risen recently, although not necessarily everywhere.

2-star denotes a comfortable hotel, where you can expect a private bathroom.

❂ 3-star qualifies a very comfortable hotel, where a private bathroom and toilet are standard, and breakfast is served in the rooms if you so wish.

4-star is granted to high-class hotels. Some have long been internationally famous, such as the **Ritz,** place Vendôme, 75001; the **Crillon,** place de la Concorde, 75008; **the George V**, avenue George V, 75008; and the **Hilton Hotel Paris,** avenue de Suffren, 75015.

5-star is granted to only a very few deluxe hotels that the French call *palaces.* **The Meurice,** rue de Rivoli, 75001, was the German headquarters during World War II.

As they are in greater demand, there are more 2- and 3-star hotels throughout the city.

Breakfast

As a rule, all hotels provide breakfast, but generally only 3-star and above offer room service. The price of breakfast is quoted separately from that of the room and though you are expected to, you are not obliged to have it.

In most cases, hotels offer a 'continental' breakfast, which usually includes tea, milk, coffee, or chocolate, a *baguette* (crisp French bread) with butter and jam or honey, and croissants.

Some hotels now offer an English- or American-style breakfast to guests on payment of a supplement.

Prices

By Western standards, Parisian hotels are fairly reasonably priced on the whole, although they are more expensive than in French provincial towns. Charging by the room rather than per person is still common practice (some hotels have family rooms for parents with one or two children).

Prices are not controlled, and so vary a lot according to the time of year, and even from one hotel to another within a given official category; they can also be changed without prior notice. However, prices including tax and service charge must be displayed outside hotels, in the reception area, and in the rooms.

The easiest method of payment is by credit card, which only a few hotels in the lowest category do not accept.

Selecting a Hotel

Most people prefer central areas in order to reduce travelling times to a minimum and to be able to fully enjoy the atmosphere of the city. Most luxury hotels are in the Madeleine–Opéra–Champs Elysées area, which covers the 1st, 8th, and 9th *arrondissements*, while the Left Bank, especially the 5th, 6th, and 7th *arrondissements*, has a profusion of smaller, more relaxed, but still very comfortable, establishments. This is only a general indication and it is quite possible to find a middle- or lower-grade hotel on the Right Bank.

The convenience of central areas such as the Gare du Nord/Gare de l'Est, Pigalle, and the eastern districts should be balanced against some less attractive aspects.

Hotels in Paris are listed in a free booklet published by the Office du Tourisme et des Congrès de Paris, available with the official representative of the French tourist office in your country.

Comfort and convenience at the Hôtel Crillon, one of over 1,400 hotels in the city

Booking a Hotel

It is advisable to book in advance (preferably a month or so) all the year round, but especially between Easter and October when more tourists come to Paris. You can do so by telephone, letter, or fax. Make your preferences quite clear: a room at the back if traffic noise bothers you, a separate bathroom, or, if you don't like climbing stairs, inquire whether there is a lift or ask for a room on a lower floor. Normally, a deposit is required with your confirmation.

If you arrive in Paris without having made a reservation, the Office du Tourisme et des Congrès de Paris will be able to help you. They have a Service de Réservations Hôtelières in their main offices, located at 127 Champs Elysées 75008 Paris, *tel: 08 36 68 31 12, www.paris.touristoffice.com* open daily from 9am to 8pm, and subsidiary offices at the main stations (except the Gare St-Lazare) as well as at the Eiffel Tower (from May to September only). These act as an emergency service for immediate accommodation but they are closed on Sunday except at the Gare du Nord.

Below is a list of other organisations, *centrales de réservations hôtelières*, which deal with hotel bookings by phone or fax:

Abotél *Tel: 01 47 27 15 15; fax: 01 47 27 05 87. www.abotelparis.com*
Ely 12 12 *Tel: 01 43 59 12 12, fax: 01 42 56 24 31; www.ely2121.com*
Paris Séjour Réservation
Tel: 01 53 89 10 50; fax: 01 53 89 10 59.
Prestotel *Tel: 01 45 26 22 55; fax: 01 45 26 05 14.*

In the more up-market establishments receptionists are usually bilingual, and any hotel with 2 or more stars must by law have a receptionist speaking a second language.

Other Accommodation

Self-catering is ideal for those who wish to have complete freedom to sample French cuisine. Self-catering apartments on short-term lets, called *meublés de tourisme*, are available for a minimum of one week and for a maximum of three months. The fully furnished one- to four-room apartments are equipped with telephone, colour television and, in some cases, washing machine and dishwasher. Sheets are usually provided. Prices are lower for longer lets.

Below is a selection of agencies and organisations approved by the Office du Tourisme et des Congrès de Paris. They are usually open during normal office hours.

ABM Rent a Flat, 12 rue Valentin Haüy, 75015. *Tel: 01 45 67 04 04; fax: 01 45 67 90 15.* Métro: Ségur.
Flatotel Expo, 52 rue d'Oradour sur Glane, 75015. *Tel: 01 45 54 93 45; fax: 01 45 54 93 07.*
Métro: Porte de Versailles.
France-Ermitage, 5 rue Berrye, 75008. *Tel: 01 42 56 23 42; fax: 01 42 56 08 99.* Métro: Charles-de-Gaulle-Etoile or George V.
Immovac, 37 avenue de Lowendal, 75015. *Tel: 01 45 67 70 00; fax: 01 43 06 12 50.* Métro: Cambronne.
Paris Séjour Réservation, 90 avenue des Champs-Elysées, 75008. *Tel: 01 53 89 10 50; fax: 01 53 89 10 59.* Métro: George V.

Bed and breakfast is ideal for those who wish to get to know French people and the French way of life. There is a small membership or registration fee, and the minimum stay is two nights. Prices are quoted per person. **France Lodge** (41 rue La Fayette 75009; *tel: 01 53 20 09 09*; métro: Le Peletier) strongly advises

against last-minute reservations. For student accommodation and camping, *see p179 & p188*.

If you come to Paris by car you will encounter parking problems. Hotels with parking are generally modern blocks outside the centre, though many are located close to public car parks.

Sign of welcome at a Marais hotel

Practical Guide

Arriving

EU residents visiting France need only show a valid passport to enter the country. This applies to US citizens, Canadians, and New Zealand nationals also, providing the length of their stay does not exceed three months; a visa is required for a longer stay. Visitors from Australia need a visa whatever the length of their stay. Visas are obtainable from French embassies and consulates in your own country; apply two months in advance in case of delays.

By Air

Paris has two main airports: Charles de Gaulle, 23km northeast of the city, and Orly, 14km south.

Charles de Gaulle (*tel: 01 48 62 22 80 24 hours a day, www.adp.fr*). Roissyrail, the free airport shuttle service, takes passengers to Roissy station where they can board the RER B (train every 8 minutes) for Châtelet-les-Halles. Air France buses leave every 12 minutes to Porte Maillot, place Charles-de-Gaulle and Gare Montparnasse (from Terminal 2). Regular RATP buses run from Roissy station to Gare du Nord/Gare de l'Est (No. 350), and place de la Nation (No. 351).

Orly (*tel: 01 49 75 15 15 6am–midnight, www.adp.fr*). The new Orlyval is a fully automatic métro which operates a shuttle service (every 10 minutes from 6.30am–10.30pm, Sunday 7am–11pm) between the airport and the RER B at Antony station, then on to Châtelet-les-Halles. It is more expensive than Orlyrail, which combines the

The métro: clearly marked, clean, and efficient

airport bus shuttle service with the RER C to St-Michel-Notre-Dame (every 20 minutes; Orly–Paris: 5.45am–11.15pm; Paris–Orly: 5.50am–10.50pm). Air France buses leave every 12 minutes for Les Invalides and Gare Montparnasse. Orlybus runs every 15 minutes between 6am–11.30pm from the airport to the place Denfert-Rochereau, connecting with the RER B or the métro.

Thomas Cook Network travel locations offer airline ticket re-routing and revalidation free of charge to travellers who have purchased their tickets from Thomas Cook. Ask your Thomas Cook travel consultant for details of the local Network licensee.

By Train
The six main-line stations are within easy reach of the city centre by RER or métro:

Gare d'Austerlitz 55 quai d'Austerlitz, 75013; RER C and métro line 10.

Gare de l'Est place du 11 novembre 1918, 75010; métro lines 4 and 7.

Gare de Lyon 20 boulevard Diderot, 75012; RER A and métro line 1.

Gare Montparnasse 17 boulevard de Vaugirard 75015; métro lines 4, 12, and 13.

Gare du Nord 18 rue de Dunkerque, 75010; RER B and D and métro line 4.

Gare St-Lazare 13 rue d'Amsterdam, 75008. This station is situated in the centre, in the Madeleine/Opéra district.

Cross-Channel services from Britain arrive at Gare du Nord or Gare St-Lazare.

The *Thomas Cook European Timetable* has details of train services, including night trains, and is available from Thomas Cook branches in the UK or call (*01733*) *416477*.

By Car
Whether you arrive by *autoroute* (motorway) or *route nationale* (A road), you will meet the *boulevard périphérique*, which you can follow until you reach the *porte* (exit) closest to your destination.

Babysitter
Two reliable agencies are: **ABABA** (*tel: 01 45 49 46 46*), and **Maman Poule** (*tel: 01 45 20 96 96*).

Camping
For information contact the **Fédération Française de Camping et de Caravanning** 78 rue de Rivoli, 75004 (*tel: 01 42 72 84 08*), métro Hôtel-de-Ville.

The following are the most convenient camping sites in and around Paris: **Camping du Bois de Boulogne** (Allée du Bord de l'Eau, 75016; *tel: 01 45 24 30 00;* métro: Pont-de-Neuilly, then bus No. 244); **Camping International** (1 rue Johnson, 78600 Maisons-Lafitte; *tel: 01 39 12 21 91*; 15 minutes from Paris by RER A); **Camping du Parc Etang** (Base de Loisirs, 78180, Montigny-le-Bretonneux; *tel: 01 30 58 56 20;* RER C to St-Quentin-en-Yvelines); **Camping du Parc de la Colline** (route de Lagny, 77200 Torcy; *tel: 01 60 05 42 32*; RER A to Torcy-Marne-la-Vallée, then bus 421).

Gloved traffic police keep things moving

Children

Children under 4 years travel free on the Paris transport network, and under-18s get into national museums free. Shoppers will find that babyfood and disposable nappies are cheaper in large supermarkets than in pharmacies.

Climate

Paris enjoys a temperate climate, with moderate rainfall and a good deal of sunshine in spring, summer, and even winter. July and August are hottest, January and February the coldest. The rainiest season is autumn.

Crime

Do not leave anything of value visible in your car. Watch your bag in crowded places. Be particularly careful in areas such as the Forum des Halles, the Gare du Nord, and Gare de l'Est districts, including the 18th *arrondissement*, and Strasbourg St-Denis. The métro is safe during the day, but, along with the RER, should be avoided after 11pm.

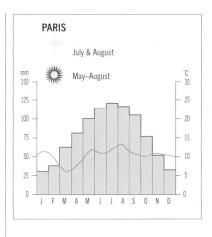

PARIS

July & August

May–August

Weather Conversion Chart
25.4mm = 1 inch
°F = 1.8 x °C + 32

Boules in the Bois de Vincennes

Paris Observatory, centre of research

Driving

Make sure you take your car registration papers and driving licence; an international driving licence is not usually necessary. Your insurance policy covers you for third-party, but if you want comprehensive cover you will need an International Insurance Certificate (green card). In addition, motoring organisations in your own country have accident/breakdown schemes.

If you hire a car, make sure your domestic insurance covers you for third-party liability; if not, you should obtain top-up cover from your insurers.

Road signs are international. There are four grades of fuel: *gasoil* sometimes spelt *gazolle* (diesel), super (98 octane), *sans plomb* (95 octane unleaded), and super *sans plomb* (98 octane unleaded).

A detailed map of Paris which clearly indicates one-way streets is essential. Wearing seat belts is compulsory, and

Conversion Table

FROM	TO	MULTIPLY BY
Inches	Centimetres	2.54
Feet	Metres	0.3048
Yards	Metres	0.9144
Miles	Kilometres	1.6090
Acres	Hectares	0.4047
Gallons	Litres	4.5460
Ounces	Grams	28.35
Pounds	Grams	453.6
Pounds	Kilograms	0.4536
Tons	Tonnes	1.0160

To convert back, for example from centimetres to inches, divide by the number in the third column.

Men's Suits

UK		36	38	40	42	44	46	48
Rest of Europe	46	48	50	52	54	56	58
US		36	38	40	42	44	46	48

Dress Sizes

UK		8	10	12	14	16	18
France		36	38	40	42	44	46
Italy		38	40	42	44	46	48
Rest of Europe		34	36	38	40	42	44
US		6	8	10	12	14	16

Men's Shirts

UK	14	14.5	15	15.5	16	16.5	17
Rest of Europe	36	37	38	39/40	41	42	43
US	14	14.5	15	15.5	16	16.5	17

Men's Shoes

UK	7	7.5	8.5	9.5	10.5	11
Rest of Europe	41	42	43	44	45	46
US	8	8.5	9.5	10.5	11.5	12

Women's Shoes

UK	4.5	5	5.5	6	6.5	7
Rest of Europe	38	38	39	39	40	41
US	6	6.5	7	7.5	8	8.5

speed is limited to 50kph throughout the city, but 80kph on the *périphérique*.

The *priorité à droite* (giving way to traffic approaching from the right) is strictly observed and bus lanes should be kept clear.

Parking can be a problem and you may decide to leave your car in a long-term car park (ask at your hotel). In the city centre, there are parking spaces along the kerb marked *payant* and ticket distributors nearby; the maximum time allowed is two hours (traffic wardens are very efficient). However, parking is free almost everywhere during August. There are also underground car parks at Notre-Dame, Hôtel de Ville, Les Halles, Concorde, etc.

All the major international car hire companies are represented in Paris; they operate from a central booking telephone number, but you can pick up a car from various points in the city.
Autorent *Tel: 01 45 54 22 45.*
Avis *Tel: 01 46 10 60 60.*
Europcar *Tel: 01 30 43 82 82.*
Hertz *Tel: 01 47 88 51 51.*
There is also the internet-only car rental company, *www. rentacar.com* Most of these also offer chauffeur-driven cars.
London Cab in Paris (*tel: 01 43 70 00 62*), has a fleet of London taxis with bilingual drivers on demand!

Electricity

Supply is 220 volts. Two-pin continental plugs can be used everywhere, even in power sockets.

Embassies

Australia 4 rue Jean Rey, 75015.
Tel: 01 40 59 33 00.

Refuel at *un poste à essence*

Canada 5 rue de Constantine, 75007.
Tel: 01 44 43 29 00.
Ireland 4 rue Rude, 75016.
Tel: 01 44 17 67 00.
New Zealand 7 ter rue Léonard de Vinci, 75016. *Tel: 01 45 00 24 11.*
UK 35 rue du Faubourg-St-Honoré, 75008. *Tel: 01 44 51 31 00.*
US 2 avenue Gabriel, 75008.
Tel: 08 36 70 14 88.

Emergency Numbers

Police Secours (accidents): *17*
Pompiers (fire): *18*
Samu (ambulance): *15 & 01 45 67 50 50.*
SOS Médecins (doctor): *01 43 77 77 77 & 01 47 07 77 77.*
SOS Dentaire (dentist): *01 43 37 51 00* from 8pm to midnight.
Burns *01 43 46 13 90* (children), *01 42 34 17 60* (adults).
Poison Centre *01 40 05 48 48.*
SOS Dépannage (car breakdown): *01 47 07 99 99.*
MasterCard Card Loss or Theft: *08 36 69 08 80* (freephone).
Thomas Cook Traveller's Cheque Loss or Theft: *08 00 90 83 30* (freephone) or 0044 1733 318950 (UK number, reverse charges). The Thomas Cook Worldwide Customer Promise offers free emergency assistance at any Thomas Cook Network location to Thomas Cook travellers.

Health

EU residents should obtain a form E111 to enable them to receive the same benefits as French nationals. However, as only 70 to 80 per cent of medical expenses are reimbursed, visitors to France are advised to take out a separate medical insurance. For residents outside the EU, they should obtain the relevant information from their own country.

National Holidays

On these days, administrative offices and banks are closed, as well as some monuments and museums. Some shops and hypermarkets remain open.

1 January New Year's Day
Variable Easter Monday
6th Thursday after Easter
Ascension Day
2nd Monday after Ascension Day
Whit Monday
1 May May Day
8 May Victory in Europe Day (1945)
14 July Bastille Day (National Day)
15 August Assumption Day
1 November All Saints' Day
11 November Armistice Day
25 December Christmas Day

Universal sign of frustration: no entry

Bane of drivers: vigilant traffic wardens

Quite a few shops and restaurants are closed during August.

Lost Property

36 rue des Morillons, 75015.
Tel: 01 55 76 20 20. Métro: Convention.
Open: Mon, Wed, Fri 8.30am–5pm,
Tue, Thu 8.30am–8pm.
Lost or Stolen Credit Cards:
American Express *Tel: 01 47 77 77 07.*
Diner's Club *Tel: 01 49 06 17 90.*
Eurocard, MasterCard
Tel: 08 00 90 13 87.
JCB International *Tel: 01 42 86 06 42.*
Visa International *Tel: 01 00 90 11 79.*

Media
Newspapers

There are no evening newspapers. *Le Figaro* and *Le Monde* have supplements or magazines on several days of the week, dealing with cultural events, travelling, books, economic and financial matters, etc.

There is also a profusion of publications containing the weekly radio and television programmes with comments and topical articles on stars

LANGUAGE

BASIC WORDS		**railway station**	la gare
AND PHRASES		**platform**	le quai
yes	oui		
no	non	**NUMBERS AND**	
please	s'il vous plaît	**QUANTITY**	
thank you	merci	**one**	un
excuse me	excusez-moi	**two**	deux
I am sorry	pardon	**three**	trois
good morning	bonjour	**four**	quatre
good evening	bonsoir	**five**	cinq
good night	bonne nuit	**six**	six
goodbye	au revoir	**seven**	sept
I have. . .	j'ai...	**eight**	huit
It is. . .	c'est...	**nine**	neuf
Do you speak	Parlez-vous	**ten**	dix
English?	anglais?	**a little**	un peu
I do not	Je ne comprends	**enough**	assez
understand	pas	**much/many**	beaucoup
when	quand	**too much/many**	trop
yesterday	hier		
today	aujourd'hui	**DAYS OF**	
tomorrow	demain	**THE WEEK**	
at what time. . ?	à quelle heure. . ?	**Monday**	lundi
where is. . ?	où est. . ?	**Tuesday**	mardi
here	ici	**Wednesday**	mercredi
there	là	**Thursday**	jeudi
near	près	**Friday**	vendredi
before	avant	**Saturday**	samedi
in front of	devant	**Sunday**	dimanche
behind	derrière		
opposite	en face de	**MONTHS**	
right	à droite	**January**	janvier
left	à gauche	**February**	février
straight on	tout droit	**March**	mars
car park	un parking	**April**	avril
petrol station	un poste à essence	**May**	mai
parking	stationnement	**June**	juin
prohibited	interdit	**July**	juillet
bridge	le pont	**August**	août
street	la rue	**September**	septembre
bus stop	l'arrêt du bus	**October**	octobre
underground	la station de	**November**	novembre
station	métro	**December**	décembre

and personalities; *Télérama* is one of the best. The whole range of entertainment offered by the capital is reviewed in detail by two very cheap weekly publications, issued on Wednesday – *Pariscope* and *L'Officiel des Spectacles*. Newspapers and magazines are on sale in kiosks dotted about the city as well as in *Maisons de la Presse* (newsagents), *Journaux-Tabacs* (tobacconists), and some bookshops. Most foreign newspapers are available in the centre, at railway stations, and airports.

Radio

Apart from the national stations like *France Inter* and *France Culture*, there are many local stations which broadcast on FM for the benefit of the Paris region, from *Radio Classique*, the non-stop classical music programme, to *Nostalgie*, a mixture of French songs and light music, and several ethnic stations.

Television

There are six national channels, four public and two private: *Paris Première* is devoted to Paris and its region.

Le Figaro: a long-established, conservative paper

Money Matters

Exchanging currency (notes, traveller's cheques, credit cards) is no problem in Paris; it can be done in banks all over the city or in bureaux de change.

Thomas Cook traveller's cheques can be cashed free of commission charges at any of the Thomas Cook bureaux listed on pages 189–90, and if denominated in Euros, are accepted as cash in hotels, larger restaurants, and stores. You can pay by credit card almost everywhere.

If you need to transfer money quickly, you can use the MoneyGram℠ Money Transfer service. For more details telephone Freephone *0800 897198* (in the UK).

Opening Times

Banks: 9am–4.30pm except Saturday, Sunday, and holidays.
Bureaux de Change: 6.30am–11pm at airports, 6.30am–10pm at railway stations, 10am–7pm in town. *(See pp189–90 for Thomas Cook opening hours.)*

If you find yourself short of cash outside the above opening hours, try a cash distributor. More and more now accept foreign credit cards and have easy-to-follow instructions.
Museums: national museums are closed on Tuesday, except the Musée d'Orsay, the Musée Rodin, and Versailles, which are closed on Monday. Opening hours are usually from 9am–6pm.

Paris museums are generally closed on Monday and free on Sunday (except temporary exhibitions). They are usually open from 10am–5.40pm.
Shops: most open weekdays 9am–7pm.

Some close noon–2pm, some on Monday morning. Department stores are open daily, except Sunday, from 9.30am–6.30pm, and have a late-closing day midweek. Food shops open at 7am or 8am and close around 8pm; they often close for three hours in the middle of the day. A few also open on Sunday morning.

Organised Tours
On Foot
The Direction Départementale de la Jeunesse et des Sports de Paris publishes a useful booklet about various walks around Paris (6–8 rue Eugène-Oudiné, 75013; *tel: 01 40 77 55 00)*.

By Bicycle
Several bicycle-hire companies organise trips in and around Paris. Contact:
Paris à Velo, c'est Sympa 37 boulevard Bourdon, 75004; *tel: 01 48 87 60 01*; Métro: Bastille.

By Bus
Several companies offer tours of the city and excursions to famous places such as Versailles and many others.
Cityrama 4 place des Pyramides, 75001. *Tel: 01 44 55 61 00.* Métro: Palais-Royal.
Paris Vision 214 rue de Rivoli, 75001. *Tel: 01 42 60 30 01.* Métro: Tuileries.
RATP Excursions (run by the Paris Transport Authority); departure from place de la Madeleine; for free brochure and information, *tel: 01 40 06 71 45.* Bookings can be done in advance from place de la Madeleine, (métro Madeleine) or from 53 bis quai des Grands-Augustins (métro St-Michel or Pont-Neuf).

The bus service is well organised and convenient

By Boat
There are various possibilities for cruising on the Seine and on the Canal St-Martin.
Bateaux Mouches Pont de l'Alma, 75007. *Tel: 01 40 76 99 99.* Métro: Pont de l'Alma.
Bateaux Parisiens Pont d'Iéna. *Tel: 01 44 11 33 44.* Métro: Trocadéro, Bir Hakeim.
Vedettes du Pont-Neuf square du Vert-Galant, 75001. *Tel: 01 46 33 98 38.* Métro: Pont-Neuf.
Canauxrama 5 bis quai de la Loire, 75019. *Tel: 01 42 39 15 00.* Métro: Jaurès.
Paris-Canal 21 quai de la Loire, 75019. *Tel: 01 42 40 96 97.* Métro: Jaurès.
Vedettes de Paris Port de Suffren, 75007. *Tel: 01 47 05 71 29.*

Helicopter and Hot Air Balloon Trips
Héli-France 4 avenue de la Porte de Sèvres, 75015; *tel: 01 41 45 54 95*; métro: Balard.

Pharmacies

The following remain open outside normal hours:

British and American Pharmacy
1 rue Auber, 75009.
Tel: 01 47 42 49 40. Open: daily except Sunday until 8pm. English spoken.
Métro: Opéra.

Pharmacie Anglaise
62 Champs Elysées, 75008. *Tel: 01 43 59 22 52.* Open: daily except Sunday until 10.30pm. Métro: Franklin-Roosevelt.

Places of Worship

For information contact the **Religious Information and Documentation Centre** 8 rue Ville l'Evéque, 75008.
Tel: 01 49 24 11 44. Métro: Madeleine.
Denominational churches include:
St Michael's Anglican Church 5 rue d'Aguesseau, 75008. *Tel: 01 47 42 70 88.*
Métro: Madeleine.
The American Cathedral 23 avenue George V 75008. *Tel: 01 53 23 84 00.*
Métro: Alma-Marceau.
St Joseph's English Catholic Church 50 avenue Hoche, 75008.
Tel: 01 42 27 28 56.
Métro: Charles-de-Gaulle-Etoile.
Church of Scotland 17 rue Bayard, 75008. *Tel: 01 48 78 47 94.*
Métro: Franklin-Roosevelt.
Synagogue La Victoire, 44 rue de la Victoire, 75009. *Tel: 01 45 26 95 36.*
Métro: Notre-Dame-de-Lorette.
Grande Mosquée 39 rue Geoffroy-Saint-Hilaire, 75005. *Tel: 01 45 35 97 33.*
Métro: Jussieu.

Police

The **Préfecture de Police** 7 boulevard du Palais 75004. *Tel: 01 53 71 53 36.* On the

A pharmacy located in a lovely old building

Ile-de-la-Cité is the police headquarters. There are *commissariats de police* (police stations) in each *arrondissement*. In case of emergency, *tel: 17.*

Post Offices

Bureaux de poste are open Mon–Fri 8am–7pm, Sat 8am–noon.

The main office (52 rue du Louvre, 75001; *tel: 01 40 28 20 40*; métro: Louvre-Rivoli) is open 24 hours a day, 7 days a week. The address for *poste restante* mail is: Poste Restante, 52 rue du Louvre, 75001 Paris RP, France. Stamps can also be bought in a *tabac* (tobacconist). Post boxes are yellow, free-standing, or set into a wall.

Outside rush hours, public transport is comfortable

Public Transport

The métro/RER/suburban railway/buses network is run jointly by the Régie Autonome des Transports Parisiens (RATP) and the Société Nationale des Chemins de Fer (SNCF). For general information, telephone:

RATP *Tel: 01 43 46 14 14* (between 6am and 9pm). English-speaking service: *Tel: 08 36 68 41 14.*
SNCF *Tel:* 08 36 35 35 35 (6am–10pm). Passes, available from the main tourist office, métro, RER, and railway stations, entitle visitors to use the whole network for one day *(Formule 1)*, three or five days *(Paris Visite).*

For information about the **Batobus**, *tel: 01 44 11 33 99. (Also see p21.)*

Day and night charges are indicated inside taxi cabs; a supplement is due if you board a taxi at a railway station or airport, or have more than one suitcase.

For complaints write to: **Service Taxis, Préfecture de Police,** 36 rue des Morillons, 75015 Paris.

Senior Citizens

Whatever their nationality, senior citizens are allowed a discount in some museums and places of entertainment such as cinemas, on presentation of their passport.

Sport

See pp160–63.

Allo-Sports (*tel: 01 42 76 54 54* 10.30am–5pm except weekends), gives information on sports events, clubs and associations.

Student Accommodation

Call **Federation Unie des Auberges de Jeunesse** for information *(tel: 01 44 89 87 27; fax: 01 44 89 87 10).* Several youth associations offer cheap lodging:
AJF 9 rue Chaptal, 75009.
Tel: 01 42 80 00 33.
CROUS 39 avenue Georges-Bernanos, 75005. *Tel: 01 40 51 55 55.*

Telephones

Calls from hotels are more expensive than from a post office or a telephone booth. Some of these are still coin-operated, but the majority work on a *télécarte* (phonecard) available in post offices, tobacconists, and main métro/RER stations. The Thomas Cook Rechargeable Prepaid Phonecard is an international pre-paid telephone card supported by a 24-hour multilingual customer service. Available from Thomas Cook branches in the UK, it can be recharged by calling the customer service unit and quoting your credit card number.

Numbers in France comprise 10 digits. All numbers for Paris and its outskirts begin 01. There are no area codes. To make an internal call simply dial the number. For the operator dial 13; for directory enquiries dial 12.

To make an international call, dial 00 then the country code (Australia 61, New Zealand 64, UK 44, US and Canada 1), then the area code (minus any initial 0) followed by the number. It is cheaper to call after 7pm weekdays, or after 2pm Saturday, and all day Sunday.

Thomas Cook

Thomas Cook *bureaux de change* in Paris are open seven days a week and have extended opening hours. They will cash Thomas Cook Traveller's Cheques free of commission charges and will provide emergency assistance in the case of lost or stolen Thomas Cook Traveller's Cheques. The locations asterisked also offer Money Gram^{SM}, a quick international money transfer facility. Most also sell maps.

Thomas Cook *bureaux* can be found at the following locations in Paris:

Champs Elysées 52, 73, and 125 avenue des Champs Elysées.
Montmartre 84 boulevard de Clichy*.
Rail stations Gare St-Lazare; Gare du Nord; Gare de l'Est; Gare Montparnasse.
Halles-Rivoli 194 rue de Rivoli*; 36–42 rue Rambuteau*.

Taxis are not easy to hail, so head for a taxi rank

St-Michel 4 boulevard St-Michel*.
Opéra 25 boulevard des Capucines*;
8 place de l'Opéra.
Tour Eiffel Tour Eiffel.

   Thomas Cook's website at
www.thomascook.com provides
up-to-the-minute details of Thomas
Cook's travel and foreign money
services.

Time
GMT plus 1 hour (winter), plus 2 hours
(summer).

Tipping
Service is included in cafés and
restaurants. It is customary to tip hotel
porters and chamber maids (for a
stay of several days), as well as museum
guides, usherettes in cinemas, and taxi
drivers.

Toilets
There are public toilets in department
stores, cafés, and restaurants, and coin-
operated booths on the pavements.

Tourist Offices
**Office du Tourisme et des Congrès de
Paris** 127 Champs Elysées, 75008
(*tel: 01 49 52 53 54;* open: daily
9am–8pm; métro: George V). There are
branches at all the railway stations, and
at the Eiffel Tower.
The **Mairie de Paris** has a Bureau
d'Accueil at 29 rue de Rivoli, 75004
(*tel: 01 42 76 43 43*; open: 9am–6pm;
closed: Sunday; métro: Hôtel de Ville).

Travellers with Disabilities
Ease of access to sights, museums,
theatres, and other public places in

Remember to retrieve your phonecard!

Paris is improving as the city makes a
real effort to welcome visitors with
disabilities.

   Several brochures on various aspects
of daily life are available by mail order
directly from local organisations such as:
l'Association des Paralysés de France,
Délégation de Paris, 17 boulevard
Auguste Blanqui, 75013
(*tel: 01 53 80 99 30*), and le Comité
National Français de Liaison pour la
Réadaptation des Handicapés
(CNFLRH), 236 rue de Tolbiae, 75013
(*tel: 01 53 80 66 66*).

   Access in Paris, a fully researched
guide for wheelchair users and
walkers with disabilities, is available
free from Access Projects, 39 Bradley
Gardens, London W13 8HE. It deals
with all aspects of travelling to Paris,
and how to make the most of it once
you are there.

ACKNOWLEDGEMENTS

Thomas Cook wishes to thank the photographers, picture libraries, and other organisations for the loan of the photographs reproduced in this book, to whom copyright in the photographs belongs.

CHRISTINE PEMBERTON 9, 14, 24, 36, 48, 50, 52, 64, 92, 94, 108a, 110, 158a, 175
CHRISTINE OSBORNE 10, 28, 70, 82, 108b, 144a
NEIL SETCHFIELD 18, 66, 67, 84, 89, 152, 158b
PICTURES COLOUR LIBRARY 13, 40, 46, 65, 83, 91, 93, 103, 116, 127, 130, 146
ALL SPORT 160, 161
RÉUNION DES MUSÉES NATIONAUX 85, 114
MARY EVANS PICTURE LIBRARY 30, 31
RITZ HOTEL 174
MUSÉE DU VIN 115
JYOTI M BANERJEE 132.

These pictures are held in the AA PHOTO LIBRARY and were taken by ANTHONY SOUTER back cover centre, 2, 3, 19, 27, 34a, 35, 37, 43, 44, 51, 54, 60, 61, 74, 77, 90, 99, 101, 105a, 106, 109, 111, 113, 117, 119, 121a, 137, 138a, 138b, 155a, 155b, 157, 168, 169, 170, 187b; PHILIP ENTICKNAP back cover top right 25, 75, 79b; PAUL KENWOOD 88; DAVID NOBLE 124, 125, 126, 128, 129, 135, 141, 143, 164, 165, 172; ERIC MEACHER 166a, 166b, 167a, 167b; and the remaining by KEN PATTERSON.

FOR LABURNUM TECHNOLOGIES

Design Director	Alpana Khare	**Photo Editor**	Radhika Singh
Series Director	Razia Grover	**DTP Designers**	Neeraj Aggarwal,
Editors	Madhavi Singh, Rajeev Jairam,		Harish Aggarwal
	Deepshikha Singh		

Updating and additional research on this edition was done by Alexander Housego.
Thanks to Marie Lorimer for the index.